Stand Up Paddle Instruction Book

*All the basics including flatwater,
fitness and surf paddling*

by Mitch Powers

Mariposa Publishing

Greenbrae, CA
Printed in USA
First Edition

Written by Mitch Powers
Photography by Mitch Powers, David Wells, Leigh Claxton, Joe
Garma & Francis Loziere
Cover design & layout by Mitch Powers
Email: Positiveoutlook1@hotmail.com

Acknowledgments

Many thanks go to a number of people who gave their support in different ways in the completion of this book. They posed as models, shared photos, offered insights about content, lent equipment for photo shoots, and generally provided an abundance of enthusiasm for this instructional book about a sport they get so much out of.

So thanks to: Sarah Quick, Leigh Claxton, Bob Licht, David Wells, Leo Siecienski, Cathy Chute, Joe Garma, Steve Hayward, Kate Clemens, Dan Griggs, Nick Suzuki and Francis Loziere. May the waves carry you far!

Also by Mitch Powers available on Amazon.com

First Strokes: Kayak Touring for Sit-on Top and Sit-Inside Kayaks

A Brief History of Sausalito and Richardson's Bay

The Adventures of Tory Cat! (color illustrated)

Stealing Hearts (a medieval love story)

Contents

Introduction

Stand Up Paddling (SUPing) is catching on like wildfire and hopefully you'll have a chance to experience this fast growing sport.

SUPing is another way to get on the water, enjoy nature, and benefit from a tremendous workout. The beauty of this sport is its simplicity, elegance, and quick learning curve. In the perfect world, meaning warm weather and water, all you need are board shorts for the guys, bikinis for the ladies, a board, paddle, leash and PFD (personal flotation device). It is truly that basic! And most people find it easy enough to load these light weight boards on their cars as well as carry them down to the water. Given calm conditions your first attempt at SUPing will meet with success and then you'll be hooked.

When you first hear about SUPing you'll hear about the great core workout it offers. What this means is that SUPing seriously develops the muscles so important for the strength and stability of the trunk, which in turn is the foundation for generating the bodies movement. Developing and strengthening the core muscles is critical for the serious or casual athlete, and in helping maintain a balanced functioning body. Besides this, the views from the stand up position are fantastic. Imagine gliding over a Caribbean reef and being able to see all the colorful fish and the underwater terrain.

Another benefit is that SUPing can be enjoyed on just about any body of water. The list is endless from: lakes, rivers, harbors, estuaries/bays and the ocean. You can pick and choose flatwater or advance your skills and tackle surfing and running rapids.

Flatwater SUPing is much easier than learning to surf and yet you still enjoy the simplicity of equipment and the elemental nature of being on the water.

My goal in this instructional book is to get you on board by providing all the basic tools you'll need. I start off by discussing SUP history and then get into the gear used. This covers clothing and includes a buyer and user guide for SUPs and paddles to help you choose the right equipment for purchase or when renting. From there we'll take an in-depth look at paddle strokes.

Importantly there is a section on safety. This covers strategies to deal with wind and chop as well as how to help others with rescues and towing scenarios. Since most people like the fitness aspect of SUPing I'll share ideas and specifics on SUP fitness ranging from exercises you can do on a board to yoga and interval training. There's also a section on SUP surfing so you can take this sport to the next level. Finally, I'll discuss transporting and carrying your SUP.

In general, the skills that are included in this book, if practiced, can take you from a beginner to intermediate level. The practice part is up to you but I've included lots of photos to illustrate the various topics of discussion and specific skills.

Chapter 1   Clothing and Equipment

You might have picked this book up after you've already tried SUPing for the first time. Or maybe you're doing a little research before you dive in. Either way this book will give you the information and skills to become a competent paddler.

In this chapter I'll start off with some background history on SUPing and follow up with discussions on gear: clothing, boards, paddles and a buyer and user guide.

A General History

Because humans have been paddling since before recorded history it is hard to pinpoint the ultimate origins of SUPing. From my research I find there's a general consensus about the beginnings of the modern evolution of SUPing and its Polynesia roots in Hawaii.

The Hawaiians call it *Hoe he'e nalu*. Back in the 1960s the Waikiki beach boys, like Duke and Leroy AhChoy, would stand up on big surfboards so they could take pictures of the tourists trying to surf. Other beach boys soon followed suit. The tips must have been good. They started using outrigger canoe paddles to give themselves more speed on the big boards to get to the outside break. Back in those days, instead of the term SUPing they called it *beach boy surfing*.

For a while *beach boy surfing* died out until big wave surfers on Maui like Laird Hamilton and Dave Kalama, along with the Makaha beach boys, started SUPing for exercise around the year 2000. Some of these surfers also found that SUPing was great training for tow-in surfing.

In tow-in surfing, a surfer is towed or pulled by a personal watercraft (aka Jet Ski) much like a water skier, in order to gain speed and critical positioning to catch massive waves.

It was around this time that Hawaiian surfer Rick Thomas introduced SUP to California. In 2004 at Hawaii's Buffalo Big Board surf contest there was a SUP category with about 49 competitors. Fast forward to Huntington Beach in July 2008 at the first annual Corona SUP Surf Challenge which drew top SUP surfers watched by about 100,000 people.

The rest as they say is history. They even SUP in Idaho now!

SUP Clothing

The best safety device you'll ever have is your brain. As in any outdoor activity it is all about assessing risk. Make smart decisions before you expose yourself to SUPing on any waterway. I'll talk more about safety in the *safety chapter* but know your local conditions. Talk to people, become aware of local weather patterns, water temperature, tides and currents. There's a simple equation. The colder the water and air temperatures are the more protection you should have, and the more critical good judgment becomes. There's no argument against preparing for immersion. What if you end up in the water? Are you dressed to handle the temperature or would you be at risk of getting hypothermia?

More specifically there's the *rule of 100*. Add air and water temperatures, and if they're less than 100 don't go out. Some safety advocates recommend the *rule of 110*, a more cautious combined temperature level to not go under.

The learning curve with most sports that are out in the elements generally means that over time you'll expose yourself to more challenging conditions. This goes with SUPing and somewhere along the way you'll end up in the water.

To make things simpler let's break down the clothing categories.

Basic Clothing To Paddle In

PFD: Personal flotation device. A SUP is considered a *vessel* by the Coast Guard and PFDs are required. Besides, it's simply a smart thing to wear. Your choice should be a Type III Coast Guard approved PFD. Worst case scenario you get caught in conditions that deteriorate. You've been falling off your board in the wind and chop, your energy level is plummeting and you end up getting separated from your board.   With

diminished energy the PFD will keep you afloat and provide some warmth. The same if you're injured. Your chances of survival are therefore greater. The problem is that with the sex appeal image of SUPing no one wants to wear them. And legally you don't have to. According to the Coast Guard the PFD just has to be *onboard*. Yeah, I understand a bikini with a PFD on just isn't the best ensemble and ruins those tan lines. That said you should get past this barrier and wear your PFD. When you need it you need it, and fumbling around to unhook it from the top of your board wastes precious time and energy. Concerned about looks? Don't worry. The SUPing industry knows about image and they are developing more and more styles of fanny pack PFDs. It's a compromise that offers "convenience, comfort and compliance, but true safety is wearing a Type III PFD."

You'll see an example of a fanny pack style PFD in the above photo. It's inflated by a CO_2 cartridge via pulling a tab. There is also a manual inflation nozzle. The photo shows the wearer with the fanny pack against the back. In reality, to deploy the PFD the wearer must spin this around to the front as the PFD goes around the neck before inflation. But most people wear the "pack" backside as the pressure against the stomach is uncomfortable.

Board Leash: If you fall off your SUP it will keep you from getting separated from the board. There are many types of leashes of course, but generally you have coiled or uncoiled leashes. For flatwater SUP activities I would choose the coiled version because it is less likely to drag in the water, and you don't move up and down on your board like in surfing so stepping on the coiled versus the flat

style leash is not an issue. Generally, you should use a leash that is as long as or slightly longer than your board. Therefore you'll find most SUP leashes to be 10-12 feet long. Too short and you might get hit by the board on the recoil.

The diameter of a SUP leash is also thicker than the ones used for the smaller and lighter surfboards. SUP leashes start at 5/16ths inch and go up from here.

Keep in mind, a good leash for SUP surfing is more critical than one used for flatwater because there'll be more torque on the leash when you wipe out. You should have a good strong leash because you don't want your leash snapping and crashing into someone. Nor do you want to be forced to make that long swim to retrieve it.

Synthetic tops: Maybe you've heard the expression "cotton kills." Yes a little dramatic but in colder environments if your tops and bottoms get wet and they're made out of cotton you'll stay cold. If you are in the Caribbean with water temperatures in the high 60s plus, and air temps in the 80s plus, cotton is a

good way to go. You'll enjoy the cooling effect without any danger. For colder weather choose materials that we call "quick dry." These are synthetic materials that are basically types of nylon like polypropylene and capilene that keep you warmer than cotton and often have properties that wick away dampness from your skin. And they simply dry quicker. Most likely you have a synthetic short or long sleeved shirt in your closet. Even better, buy one with a high sun protection factor.

Synthetic bottoms: Same materials as described above. You can wear board shorts or bathing trunks, shorts, bikini bottoms and so forth. If you are looking for more sun protection on the lower half get something light weight and non-restrictive that covers your calves.

Wetsuits: It's best to be dressed for immersion. The one exception is if you are in a hot climate. With time you'll learn to weigh your abilities/limits against weather conditions to assess risk and make safe choices about paddling clothing on any given day.

There are a variety of types of wetsuits made from neoprene to

Full body wetsuit

Farmer John wetsuit

choose from. The basics range from a Farmer John style wetsuit to a full body wetsuit.

Farmer John style wetsuits like all wetsuit types come in a number of thicknesses. Typically you'll have 2-3mm thick Farmer Johns. Generally, except in colder conditions this is a good range. Farmer John style wetsuits are sleeveless so there is unrestricted range of motion for paddling. They also come in shorty style which means they end just above the knee rather than covering the full leg.

Call the Farmer John style a compromise. It's not as hot or restrictive as a full body wetsuit. But it's not a great choice for SUP surfing in colder waters because every time you wipeout you get a flush of cold water through the open shoulders and neckline. This means your core temperature gets colder faster. In this scenario a full body wetsuit is the choice. Today's full body models are often designed with thinner neoprene around flexion points like the knees and shoulders for ease of motion.

A tight fit is critical since wetsuits work by trapping a small amount of water heated by your body temperature. A loose wetsuit means too much water which your body can't heat enough to keep you warm.

Similar to surfing, if you are in flatwater but fall off your board you get that same rush of cold water. But in flatwater you're less likely to lose your balance or fall in that frequently. Therefore the Farmer John is an acceptable compromise.

For options some people will buy a Farmer John and also a separate neoprene jacket. So this is a two piece solution that offers flexibility. On colder days wear the jacket over the Farmer John for more warmth and it will stop that cold rush of water when you fall off your board practicing that pivot turn.

Drysuits: This is a big ticket item given the sticker price of $500 for a basic style and $1,000 plus for top of the line. Just as the name implies, if the quality and fit are good, a drysuit will keep you dry even if you spend a lot of time in the water. You are basically wearing a windproof/waterproof shell with neck, wrist and ankle gaskets that seal tight against your skin to keep all water out. Temperature adjustment is via layering underneath with synthetic tops/bottoms. Super cold water and you might be wearing thick fleece pants and shirt under your drysuit. This is great gear for SUPing those cold winter rivers or lakes. Surfers are not likely to wear drysuits if they can avoid them because they are baggy and create more drag than form fitting neoprene wetsuits. They can also hold air pockets which makes it difficult to dive down to escape a crushing wave or a leaky drysuit can become an anchor. In colder surf SUPing conditions a surfer might put on a 5mm wetsuit for additional warmth.

What's great to know is that with the right gear there's no reason you can't have a blast paddling year-round.

Paddling jackets: A long sleeve nylon coated paddling jacket could serve as a cooler version of the neoprene jacket discussed above. Good paddling jackets come with a method to cinch up around the neck, wrists and waist. You can get short sleeve or long sleeve jackets. They are generally wind and waterproof and either non-breathable or breathable (Gore-Tex).

Depending on conditions, for example, if it's sunny but just a little chilly you could wear a paddling jacket over your synthetic shirt along with your board shorts. If you're just getting into the sport and don't want the expense of another piece of trendy gear that old windbreaker in your closet will suffice.

Sun protection: As a fair skinned member of the species that's had his share of sun damage I'm a big advocate for covering up. So don't forget your hat, sunscreen and sunglasses to start. Baseball caps don't offer much sun protection for the neck, face or ears and a visor offers even less in terms of the top of the head. Yep, better than nothing but consider investing in a broad brimmed hat that will hold up against the wind. A retention strap with a barrel lock will help keep your hat from shifting backwards on your head. If you want to look cool then a stiff brimmed straw hat will give you that casual day in the Caribbean sun look. Remember the sun reflects off the water so you get more sun exposure than on land.

Other Clothing Options: I think by now it's obvious that clothing choices are varied and dependent on weather conditions, your personal skills, comfort and location of SUP activity. Here are a few more things to consider.

Paddling gloves: Paddling gloves with three quarter fingers and reinforced inner thumbs (wear point) are a great way to protect your hands not only against any chaffing from your paddle but also offer critical sun protection on the part of your body that receives some of the highest sun exposure during your life time—the top of your hands. They also offer some warmth on cooler days.

Footwear: In mild climates most people go barefoot. There's a nice connected feeling with your bare feet on the pliable traction pads that most boards come with. But if you're SUP surfing or paddling in colder weather you might want to wear a pair of booties. Additionally, booties can help relieve foot cramping by providing compression. If you're paddling rivers, lakes or any body of water, and have to navigate across rocky terrain to get there, some kind of water shoe that easily strains water is a must for foot protection. Even Teva's or Chaco's, sandals with good support and heel straps, can give you a level of protection in non-sandy beach environments. Keep in mind thicker soled footwear will raise your center of gravity.

Stand Up boards-A Buyer and User Guide

This section is to help give you a better understanding of SUPs in terms of designs, materials, terminology and choosing a board. In conjunction with this the best recommendation I can give you is try out a number of different boards at a rental outlet, demo days or via friends. To understand the basics the learning curve is quick. If you can only purchase one board it should be designed to work in the environment you paddle in most of the time.

SUP materials and designs

The majority of boards start out with a foam core like EPS (expanded polystyrene). The problem with EPS is that there is air between the "cells" so if you ding your board water can get between these cells and damage the foam core. A better core is made with what is called *fused-cell* EPS and has watertight construction.

The lightest boards have a foam core and are wrapped in fiberglass. The high end version of this uses carbon fiber to replace the fiberglass and is even lighter and more expensive.

The rigidity or stiffness of your basic EPS foam block comes from fiberglass or wooden laminates. In addition, the foam core is waterproofed with a sealant.

You can also find a SUP with a foam core wrapped with a wood veneer. There are stiff all-foam boards, great for the kids, plastic boards and finally inflatable SUPs.

The inflatable SUPs are great for people traveling or with limited storage space. You can actually roll these up. Basic inflatables take about 12 PSI with high end inflatables (much stiffer) taking up to 30 PSI. Sectional foam core and fiberglass SUPs are another good way to go if space is limited in car or home. These sectional SUPs have rods to bring the sections together and a method for tightening and holding the sections in place.

Generally, there are two different styles of hulls either displacement or planning. A displacement hull cuts through the water and can reach higher speeds whereas a planning hull rides over the water like a surfboard.

SUP terminology

Nose: This is the front of the board and nose shapes vary. A

wide nose means more flotation and rides over the water better. This is good for SUP surfing. A pointed or narrow nose tends to cut through the water.

Tail: Like it sounds the tail is the back of the board. Tail designs come from surfboards as do most design elements of SUPs. The two classic designs are the *Pin Tail* and the *Square Tail*, and departures from these styles are simply variations of them.

Generally speaking, SUPs will have either a rounder tail or a more square tail. A round tail or the more extreme Pin Tail has less surface volume, and hence the tail sinks into the wave offering more stability and smoother turns in big waves and higher speeds. A square tail is better for small to mid-size waves in that the greater tail volume offers more stability and lift, and it's easier to make snappy or pivotal turns.

Rocker: This refers to the curvature of the hull from nose to tail. A board that has more rocker will turn quicker. A SUP used for surfing tends to have more rocker than let's say a SUP used for racing. Racers are concerned with forward speed and want more of the board in the water at all times. A longer waterline translates to more speed. For flatwater paddling, a lot of rocker is also bad because the board doesn't track well, and the wind will swing the board side to side.

Rails: This is the edges or sides of the board. Just like most design aspects of a SUP board there are many variables related to the performance characteristics you're looking for and can handle. If you want more of a recreational type SUP you'll go for thicker rails and hence gain greater stability.

Deck: This is basically the top of the board on which you stand. Most SUP decks come with a deck pad for traction. Some deck pads "lip up" near the tail which allows your foot to really grab the board when doing maneuvers like pivot turns where one foot is behind the other in surfer stance. If your board does not have a deck pad for traction and comfort you can buy a kit and adhere your own. In lieu of this grab some surf wax for grip.

Carrying handle: One distinction SUPs have over surfboards is they tend to be bigger in terms of width and depth. Therefore most recent SUP models have a built-in handle, set about mid-way in the center of the board. A properly placed handle should be at the balance point of the board for ease of carrying. Being the balance point means it also marks where you should kneel or stand on your SUP. Boards that don't come with a built-in handle sometimes come with an attached handle strap. You can also purchase after-market suction cup or glue on handles.

Leash plug: This is usually built into the board towards the tail end. This is what the leash attaches to. There are kits to add one if your board doesn't come with it. Some boards come with two plugs offering a more secure attachment between leash and SUP.

Deck pad lips up for extra control

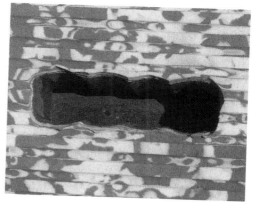

Deck straps and deck bungee systems: Yes you can actually carry gear on your SUP. This could be a drybag with camping gear or just extra layers and lunch for an extended day paddle. Some SUPs come with extra deck plugs towards the front of the board along with bungee cord type straps under which you can secure dry bags and other equipment or simply your PFD. There are kits you can purchase if your board doesn't come with this set up.

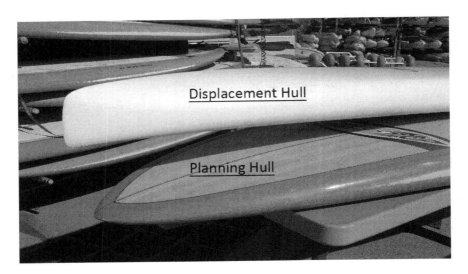

Displacement Hull

Planning Hull

Bottom or hull: Typically you'll see several hull design styles. The most prevalent is a planning style hull where the bottom is relatively flat. Another style, used primarily for racing is called a displacement hull. This type of hull tends to be more rounded and has less "wetted surface" touching the water at a given time. This is turn translates into less friction and hence more speed. It also makes for a tippier board.

Beyond these two main hull types you have many variations. For example, you might have a SUP which has a V-shape at some point and then flattens out. Some SUPs even have a concave type hull design that supposedly holds the water and creates lift. More lift and you get less drag or resistance.

Fins: Most recreational and racing SUP boards use one large fin under the rear tail but SUPS can have 1-4 fins depending on the use. For example, if you are SUP surfing you might have the one large fin in the center with two smaller side fins. This is a classic pattern and some call it the 2 + 1 fin set up, the tri-fin or more popular "thrusters". The larger fin keeps the board stable and holds the tail down. The side fins stop sideways slippage but also provide a pivot point for turning. Added to this is that there's usually room

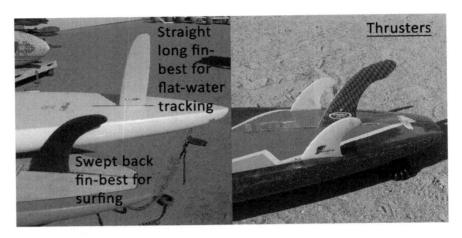

to move your fin or fins forward or back in the fin slots which effects performance.

In general, if you move the center fin forward you get more turning power. Move it back further and you get better tracking and stability. As you can imagine there are all sorts of shapes and sizes for fins with their own relative characteristics. Common lengths for a single central fin is 8-10 inches, however if you were doing a serious downwind run you might have a fin up to 15 inches. A straight long fin with a wide *chord* (depth from front to back) is best for tracking in flatwater. A shorter swept back fin is better for surfing.

Choosing a Board

Grab yourself a cold one and let's sit back and discuss this. As I stated in my introduction SUPing at its most elemental is simple. If you just want to try it, all you have to do is go to an outfitter that rents boards. They'll give you a stable board and the right sized paddle, show you the basic strokes and off you go. And yes you should start out on flatwater on a calm day.

But eventually you're going to want to address the question of what really is the right board for you whether you continue renting or want to buy one. The reality is that different boards are shaped and sized for different types of paddling such as flatwater, racing or surfing. So ultimately you'll need to figure out what type of paddling you'll be doing and match this with your athletic abilities, location and desires all of which just might be in conflict. But let's not worry about this right now but instead look at some general concepts.

11 feet
32 inches wide
5.1 inches depth
stable all around SUP

14 feet
30 inches wide
5 inches at max
faster, tippier

Volume: This is a catch all term and is a function of length, width, thickness and shape. The more volume a board has the more weight it can handle. Volume is what floats you while paddling. Given benign conditions if the volume is right for your body type and abilities you won't be swimming.

Length: SUPs are usually 9-15 feet in length. Longer means faster and a straighter line. Shorter equates to slower but easier to turn. If you're into SUP surfing you'll go for a shorter board.

Width: These boards tend to be 28-33 inches wide. Width is the key factor in a board's volume in terms of creating stability. The wider the board the more stable. A wide board is a great idea for big and tall people who need a more stable platform.

Depth: This refers to the thickness of the board and they tend to range from 4-6 inches thick. In summary, a thick wide board that has length would be the most stable platform.

SUP Chart

Here's a chart to give those of you who want it more guidance. This chart comes straight from one SUP retailer I did research on. This chart is oriented towards those using a SUP on relatively flatwater or for recreational SUPing.

BEGINNER	ADVANCED
Weight: 120-150 lbs Length: 10' 6"-11' Width: 28-30"	Weight: 120-150 lbs Length: 9-10' 6" Width: 26-26.5"
Weight: 160-190 lbs Length: 11' Width: 29-32"	Weight: 160-190 lbs Length: 9'6"-10'6" Width: 27-28"
Weight: 200-230 lbs Length: 11'-11'6" Width: 29-32"	Weight: 200-230 lbs Length: 10'-11' Width: 28-28.5"
Weight: 240-270 lbs Length: 11'6"-12' Width: 32-34"	Weight: 240-270 lbs Length: 11'-11'6" Width: 29.5-31.5"
Weight: 280+ lbs Length: 12' Width: 36"	Weight: 280+ lbs Length: 12' Width: 32"

Personally, based on my experience teaching beginners, I'd tweak this chart a bit and err on the side of longer and wider for the taller/bigger people. For example, for a 6 footer that weighed more than 190lbs I'd suggest: length 11ft.+, width 32in.+ and thickness 5in.+. You get my drift?

Keep in mind that the flatwater or recreational SUP board you use or buy can work in the surf and on rivers. It's just as you advance your skills you'll probably end up getting a board that is more tuned into the conditions you find on that river or in the surf.

Racing is of course another activity and the above applies to your initial forays into the race scene. But eventually you'll want to get a displacement hull racing SUP, and one that is longer and narrower than your recreational SUP. I'll talk a little more about these types of boards in the SUP fitness chapter.

SUP Paddles- A Buyer and User Guide

Lots of variables here but we'll stick to the basics to help you figure things out. Just keep in mind once again that where you are now and where you will be are two different things. Your interest, abilities and needs related to SUPing will evolve and thus so will your equipment. Eventually, if you branch out into surfing and racing, you might end up with a quiver of paddles. Meanwhile, for your first paddle, as one SUP shop owner says, "splurge on the paddle and skimp on the board if you must." A good paddle can greatly enhance your enjoyment of SUPing.

Types of Materials

The materials listed below can also be combined to make up your paddle. For example, you could have a fiberglass blade and a plastic shaft.

Carbon Fiber: This is the lightest and strongest material for a paddle with both the shaft and the blade made of carbon. Carbon is extremely stiff so there is less flex and hence more energy transfer. It's also the most expensive so you might save this high end purchase for the future when you actually know what you're doing.

Fiberglass: This is a step down from carbon but still offers a very light responsive type paddle. If you need to cut the price down you might get a nice glass blade with a plastic shaft.

Wood: This type of material makes for a warm looking paddle that's nice to the touch. There's some fine and unique craftsmanship out there but generally wood is heavier.

Plastic: Paddles with both shaft and blade made of plastic are cheap and heavy relative to carbon or fiberglass. You get what you pay for but then again you don't have to pay a lot so this is an acceptable way to start out.

Aluminum: Scraping the bottom of the barrel here. You'll find some cheap paddles on the market with aluminum shafts and plastic blades. The metal is cold to the touch, and frankly not only are these paddles generally ugly but they scream out beginner.

Types of Paddles

One piece paddle: Just as the name implies. We'll talk about

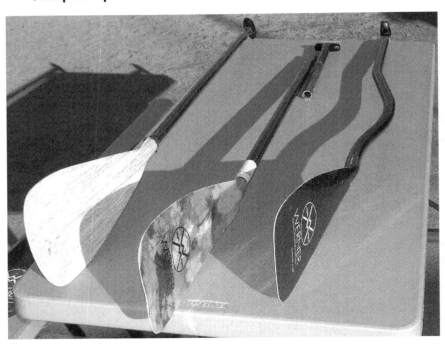

the all-important sizing of your paddle later.

Two piece adjustable break-apart paddle: This type of paddle has built in flexibility. Firstly, it breaks down into two pieces which means it might fit more easily into that small "save the planet" car of yours. Also, it can be adjusted to different lengths which means you can either lend it to a shorter/taller friend or adjust for thickness of board and activity (surf versus touring). The downside is; compared to a one piece paddle made of the same materials and general specs the adjustable will be a tad heavier and less energy-transfer efficient. But unless you're a finely tuned racer you probably won't know the difference. Just be sure and rinse it well after each use to keep the adjustment component working smoothly and free of salt, sand and grit build-up.

Three piece adjustable break-apart paddle: This is the ultimate traveling paddle that splits into three pieces but also offers adjustable lengths.

Ergonomic paddle: These are like the bent shaft paddles introduced in the kayaking world long ago designed to lessen stress on the wrists. Essentially there's a manufactured bend in the shaft where your lower hand grips it. The bend is angled to allow your wrist to remain in more of a neutral position while paddling and hence creating less stress on the joint. This bend also gives you a little more forward reach which could help distance racers. Those who own these types of paddles and paid the extra money are of course its biggest advocates. That said it does have its place and undoubtedly works. Anyone with a history of carpal tunnel syndrome, tendinitis or spending too much time on the keyboard might consider this style. Expect to pay a little more for the bend.

Paddle Terminology

There's some variation in the terminology used to describe parts of a paddle but keep in mind it's a young industry scrambling for definition. Starting from top to bottom:

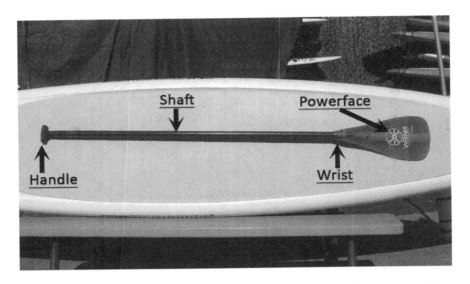

Paddle handle: This is where your top hand grips the paddle. Handles come in different contours but these various shapes, in theory, allow your hand a "good" grip. So you might have shapes that are oval, ball-like or a T-grip. The T-grip seems to be the most popular. Some handles are angled as they insert into the shaft which is an engineering design to help keep your wrist in more of a neutral position as you apply force to lessen wrist irritation. Basically the handle or grip should feel comfortable.

Paddle shaft: Earlier we talked about different types of materials that make up paddles. The paddle shaft, the section between the handle and the blade inherently has some flex depending on the material it's made of. In general, most paddlers want a shaft that offers a little flex and is light. The flex gives some relief to your joints, tendons and muscles.

Paddle shoulder, elbow, ferrule or wrist: I've heard all four for describing the section where the shaft meets the blade. My preference is to use the "wrist" terminology. Take a look at a typical SUP paddle, and as you sight down the shaft to the blade you'll see that the blade is slightly angled in one direction or bent at the wrist. When executing a forward stroke the forward angle of the blade

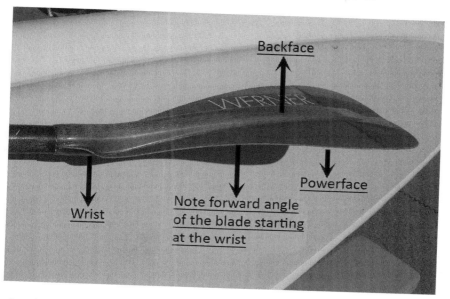

should be reaching in front of you. This may seem counterintuitive, and thus I see countless beginners without instruction paddling with the blade moving through the water backwards. Think of it this way. With the blade angled forward you can incrementally extend forward the "catch" or where the blade meets the water. This lengthens your stroke in a positive manner. Then as your paddle/blade comes towards your hip the blade holds the water in a more vertical position for longer which increases efficiency or forward drive. And most importantly as the blade exits the water, you are not lifting water. This would happen if you were paddling with the forward blade angle facing the rear.

Paddle blade: Blades come in different shapes and sizes. There are all sorts of engineering theories behind designs but I'm going to leave that to the techies to obsess over. The typical blade shape looks a bit like a tear drop. Where the wrist meets the blade the blade tends to be narrow. In part, this is because a good paddle stroke means you are driving the paddle blade close to the rail (edge) of the SUP which this allows without a lot of banging going on. From here the blade widens to give you some meat to plant in

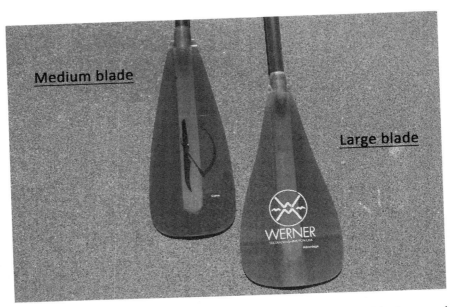

Medium blade

Large blade

WERNER
SULTAN WASHINGTON USA

the water. Ideally you'll try different paddles and one blade type/ shape will start to feel right.

When executing a forward stroke the side of the blade facing you is called the powerface. The reverse side might be called the backface, non-powerface or off-side.

Blade sizing is a little easier to tackle. The bike analogy I read works well. A big paddle blade (larger surface area) is like the low gears on a bike. If you stand up out of the saddle and pump the big gears they'll give you power and speed. However, unless you are a sprinter you'll tire quickly over distance. Therefore it depends on what type of paddling you are doing? Sprinters might want a bigger blade. Surfers would want a smaller blade which allows for a quick succession of strokes for turning/angling maneuvers. A tall medium sized blade for SUP tourers and most SUP paddlers is probably the best choice. Although if you have a "petite" frame you might go for a small blade size. To fine tune the right shape and size of blade let your SUP store or outfitter help you.

Paddle Length: The two most frequently asked questions from beginners are what size board to start out with and what's the right paddle length? I'll tackle the second question in this section but keep in mind there are a lot a variables. What do I mean by this? If you have a thicker board it raises you higher off the water and hence you'd need a slightly longer paddle than when on a thinner board. And some people have longer arms than others. Also, SUP flatwater paddlers, surfers and racers all use different paddle lengths. In general, if the SUP paddle is too short for you, you probably have to lean forward more and reach to plant the whole blade or inversely if too long it's harder, and more tiring on your joints/muscles and overextends the stroke.

From all my research here's what I've come up with. Firstly, some of the major players, that being paddle manufacturers and paddlers, have different ideas on this subject. Who would have guessed? Sit back and pop open another cold one while everyone pontificates.

Secondly, if you want to cut to the chase with one simple answer here it is. Grab a paddle, place it at your side and extend your arm straight up. If the paddle handle fits comfortably in your palm (not your extended finger tips) with the tip of the paddle blade still touching the ground you've got yourself a paddle. Now go out there and have some fun!

From this starting point, which for many of you is all you need, we can get a little more esoteric. The paddle length sizing I give you for surfing and flatwater touring below comes from a general consensus of various articles I've read. Like I said before not everyone agrees but enough people do follow the guidelines I list to give these specs credibility. And as they say we're only talking inches here.

For SUP surfing you'll pick a paddle length that is 6-8 inches above your height. If flatwater touring is your main focus, then go to 8-10 inches above height.

However, if you are racing you'll find conflicting information. Many writers recommend 10-12 inches above your height, but more and more I'm reading the contrary opinion that the racer's paddle length should be shorter than the typical touring paddle. Flatwater touring paddlers tend to have more of an upright stance versus racers that exaggerate the forward crunch. A racer is working much harder and a shorter paddle puts less stress on those hard working joints. So I recommend a paddle length somewhere between surfing and touring lengths. Like I mentioned before, if you think you'll be doing all these different SUPing activities an adjustable paddle might be the way to go.

Chapter 2   Paddle Strokes & Getting Started

Boards will come and go but the true art of the SUP is found in the grace with which you move your board.

The basic strokes are the forward, reverse and turning strokes. With these elementary strokes you can start paddling right away. In fact, if you're anxious to get on the water and already have the basics you can skip ahead in this chapter to the section on "getting on the water." Later you can come back and refine your technique.

After discussing the basic strokes we'll take a look at a variety of additional strokes and techniques for controlling your SUP. As with anything time and focus will help you master your technique. You can do this yourself but I am also an advocate of beginners at least investing in a couple lessons with a qualified instructor. I say qualified because having a friend coach you is usually a one way ticket to forming bad habits.

Finally, I'll wrap up this section with a discussion on actually getting on the water with a few handy suggestions. Please note for illustrative purposes, many of the paddle stroke shots show the blade partially out of the water. This is so you can see the angle of the paddle blade and which side is active (powerface vs. backface). Normally for most strokes the blade is fully immersed.

The Forward Stroke (Hawaiian Style)

Before we get into the dynamics of this stroke we need to talk about basic theory and hand position on the paddle. The paddle is a lever and your torso (upper body and hips) are more powerful than your arms. Thus we want to engage the torso to transfer energy through your arms to the paddle. The paddle itself has a fulcrum point which happens to be where the lower hand is placed on the shaft.

In terms of hand placement on the paddle. You have your lower hand and your top hand. If you are paddling on the right side of the board your lower hand is the right one. So how wide is your grip? Wrap one palm around the handle and the other on the shaft. Place the paddle on top of your head and spread your hands far

enough apart so that your forearms or elbows are at ninety degrees. This is the proverbial general rule of thumb. To help you keep your lower hand positioned correctly you can wrap a piece of tape around the paddle shaft. Also, as you paddle keep a loose grip to avoid hand/wrist/forearm fatigue caused by what is called the *death grip*.

One other thing. Your stance on the board is important. You need to find the center balance point of your board. Some boards come with an inset hand grip on the mid top deck for carrying the board. This is usually the mid-point or where you should stand with your feet side to side at shoulder width. Allow for a little bend in the knees. Remember your feet form a foundation and connection to the board which helps transfer your paddling energy to move the board through the water.

The Catch: Starting out on the right side. Rotate the right side of your torso forward, leading with your right hip, and fully extend your lower arm as your paddle reaches for the catch (insert point). As the blade hits the catch swing your top hand over your lower hand in vertical alignment. Some paddlers refer to this as stacking the hands. Therefore the top hand is also over the water not the board.

The blade enters the water just off the rail of the SUP. Crunch your torso forward a bit and your top hand will push down on the paddle. The blade should be fully immersed at the catch. Keep both arms relatively straight although I suggest a slight bend in the upper arm elbow rather than fully extended as this reduces strain and shock to the shoulder and elbow joints.

You can mark the catch position with a piece of tape on your board to make sure you fully extend your paddle forward. (Note: The most powerful part of the stroke is at the catch position not when the paddle is close to the exit position.) The paddle should

The Catch

Power Phase

The Exit

Recovery Phase

enter quietly not plopping, which is caused by over reaching. Plopping tends to raise the SUP nose and sink the tail, reducing forward speed.

The Power Phase: More or less simultaneous to your blade hitting the catch and your forward crunch start rotating your torso (crunch and rotate) by twisting the right side of torso backwards while the left side rotates forward. Many SUP experts talk about planting or anchoring the blade in the water and pulling the board forward of the initial catch position rather than pulling the paddle backwards through the water. I find this a hard concept to grasp. But if it helps, imagine that immediately upon hitting the catch the water instantly hardens like solid concrete. You can't move the paddle but you can use it as a lever to pull your board forward. This is also how the pros talk about an efficient kayak stroke. So those with kayaking and canoeing backgrounds will find a lot of crossover in terms of theory and technique.

Remember the entire blade face should be immersed in the water and stay positioned traveling along the edge of the rail where the wrist of the paddle is adjacent to the rail. By maintaining a vertical stroke, where the top hand is above the lower hand and the top hand is also positioned over the water, you'll get the most efficient stroke. This also helps keep the SUP moving in a straight direction. Finally, when you have an effective forward stroke there should not be a lot of side to side movement of the board.

The forward stroke I am discussing above is ideal in conditions where a paddler feels stable and in control. For most of us this means in flatwater on a stable board. There are reasons to modify this stroke such as dropping the top hand inwards away from the rail and downwards. For example, this will lower your center of gravity and provide more stability but also less efficiency.

Here's a tip for understanding what I mean by torso rotation and transferring this energy through your arms to the paddle. Stand on the ground with your paddle in front of you parallel to the ground, arms fully extended just below chest level. Have a slight bend in your knees. Now rotate your torso both ways initiating this from the hips. Keep your arms locked. You'll get a feeling for letting your torso do the work to swing the paddle and how your legs can be integrated. Now from this position, starting on the right side, drop your paddle in a more of a vertical stroke and reach for the catch and rotate backwards. Anyway, easy to describe but harder to execute or should I say easy for me to describe but hard for you to understand!

The Exit: Start your exit when the paddle blade is at your toes and fully exit by your ankles/hips. There is no power behind you. A clean exit is a good exit. In other words you want to minimize lifting water. There are a few options to the exit but we'll discuss the popular Hawaiian style here. To exit cleanly drop the top hand down to your left side which will cut the blade sideways out of the water. As you slice the blade out rotate the top hand grip forward so this thumb is facing forward. Your blade is now positioned to cut through the air (less resistance).

The Recovery or Return Phase: Here you are setting yourself up for your next stroke. Assuming you are still paddling on the right side wind up or rotate your torso forward on the right side with lower arm reaching forward as the blade cuts through the air. Keep the paddle blade low, just above the water for greater efficiency. At the same time the top hand should shift into a vertical position above the lower hand as you hit the catch as discussed above.

The conditions and your abilities will determine how straight your SUP travels. The basic way to control the direction of the nose of your board is to switch sides. You paddle a bit on the right side and find your board is wandering to the left. So then you switch over to the left side to chase the board back to the right. Later I'll talk about some more sophisticated ways to deal with correcting your direction.

Turning Strokes, Reverse Stroke and Stopping

Basic Forward Sweep Stroke: This one's pretty intuitive. Like the forward stroke and most of your strokes this one's also powered by the torso. Let's say you want to turn the board to the left. You'll execute a sweep stroke on the right side. Drop your top hand (left hand) to below chest level. Rotate your torso forward on the right side, fully extending your right arm. At the same time choke your lower hand up the shaft so the width between hands is now shoulder length. This will allow you to extend your paddle out further for a more powerful sweep. Hit the catch, starting close to the forward rail and then sweep the blade low and wide away from the board. I'll bend my knees more than usual so I can keep my back straight while making it easier to sweep out the paddle. Unlike the forward stroke where the paddle shaft is more or less in a vertical position here the shaft is held in more of a parallel position to the surface of the water.

For a minor turn you can sweep the blade halfway back. If you want a more extreme turn then sweep the paddle all the way back until you touch the rear rail. Switch sides and you'll turn the board to the right.

Reverse Sweep

Just as in the forward stroke there's the exit and recovery stage. Exit by slicing the paddle straight up out of the water. It helps if you think about dropping down the top hand and lifting the lower hand. As you wind up your torso during the recovery phase you can slice the blade through the air or not. If you want to slice the blade through the air rotate your top hand forward, again thumb facing the front. Therefore the powerface should be facing skyward as it slices towards the catch position.

Basic Reverse Sweep Stroke: This is basically the forward sweep stroke but in reverse. Starting on the right side rotate your torso (right side) backwards as you drop the top hand down below chest level. Position the powerface of the paddle against the rear rail and keeping the paddle low and wide, sweep the blade forward leading with the backface. Just like in the forward sweep stroke you can execute a partial or full sweep stroke. A reverse sweep stroke on the right side will swing the nose of your board to the right.

It's best to initially practice these turning strokes and frankly all the other strokes in calm flatwater. In this manner, without interference from wind or chop, you'll be able to fine tune your strokes to get the most efficient turning power.

Reverse Stroke and stopping: Especially when you are just starting out you'll be using these two strokes to keep from banging into docks, boats and other paddlers. I'm going to keep the explanations pretty simple here since it's not nearly as important to refine your backward stroke as it is the forward stroke for obvious reasons. You can back-up with your paddle in more of a vertical orientation with the blade hitting the catch behind you and coming straight forward adjacent to the rail. But if you feel a little tippy and want more stability drop the top hand downwards. This will give you a wider, less efficient but more stable reverse stroke. Switch sides as needed to keep your board backing up in a straight direction. And remember just as in a reverse sweep stroke you are leading with the backface of the paddle. Stopping your SUPs forward momentum can be as simple as planting your blade in the water just behind your hip position. This is like hitting the breaks. If you need a more casual stop then reach backwards and butter the surface of the water, and as you slow down you can dig the paddle in deeper.

Beyond the Basic Strokes

Okay so those are some basic strokes to get you up and running quickly. But now let's look at some more strokes to help you control your board and direction. The list is endless and you'll find you use some of these strokes more frequently than others.

The C-Stroke: Now we're getting sophisticated. This is a stroke that actively helps control the direction the nose of your SUP is moving while maintaining forward momentum. It is a stroke you can use as an option to simply switching sides. Let's say you're paddling along and you find the nose is wandering to the left. When you initiate your forward stroke on the right side, this time, instead of planting your blade in the usual catch position reach further away from the SUPs rail. Maybe a couple feet out. Rather than planting the blade with the powerface perpendicular to the rail, plant the blade at a 45 degree angle to the rail. Then pull your paddle towards the bow, which in turn pulls the nose to the right a bit. As you get close to the rail turn the powerface to its normal orientation and flow into a forward stroke. But as you come to the end of the stroke at your normal exit point now turn the powerface 90 degrees so it faces outward and at the same time push the paddle away from the rail. From here go into your normal recovery and repeat if necessary or return to a regular forward stroke.

I think it helps if you visualize carving a C through the water. The goal is to get to the point where this stroke feels fluid as opposed to jerky.

The J-Stroke: Here's another advanced stroke that when mastered will signal that you have certainly progressed. The J-stroke is another stroke that allows you to control the direction

C-Stroke

reach out at the catch with a 45 degree angle

turn powerface outward and complete the "C"

of your SUP without switching sides. Again let's assume you're paddling on the right side and the SUP nose is drifting to the left. Start off with a normal forward stroke but this time bring the blade past your usual exit point. Now at the end of this longer stroke turn the powerface towards the rail and then push the paddle outwards away from your board. The

J-Stroke

effect of this will be to correct the nose back to the right. From this point you go back go into your normal recovery stage to start another J-stroke or just a regular forward stroke. Like the C-stroke this J-stroke combines the elements of the forward stroke along with a corrective stroke counteracting slippage of the nose of the SUP without having to switch paddling sides.

Cross-Bow Sweep Stroke: Here's a fun stroke to try when you have more confidence in your ability to stay upright. Hold your paddle in front of you at a low angle, dropping your hands below chest level. Fully rotate your torso to the left allowing the paddle blade to cross over the nose slicing it into the water starting as far to the left of the nose as possible. Now start sweeping the paddle towards the rail and just before hitting the edge of your SUP cross over the bow and immediately catch the water on the opposite side initiating your normal sweep stroke. This is simply another way to turn the nose of your board.

The Spin Maneuver: This is a good way to turn your SUP around quickly and is most effective when your board is stationary. Do a forward sweep on one side and a reverse sweep on the opposite side. Remember to keep your paddle at a low angle to the water

Cross Bow Sweep

unlike your forward stroke and reach and sweep the blade away from your SUP on both sides, one side forward the other in reverse.

High Brace: This is a type of brace (stabilizing stroke) that tends to be used more in surf. In essence you're bracing the powerface of the blade against the water when you start to lose your balance.

High Brace
with powerface of
blade facing downward

Let's say you're suddenly tipping over to the right due to a boat wake, bay chop or small wave. Quickly drop your top hand (here it's the left one) down bringing the paddle into a low angle relative to the water. Keep your elbows tucked in close to your torso to protect your shoulders but extend your paddle out to the right, perpendicular to the board just in front of your hips. You can get a little more reach if you rotate your torso towards the bracing side. Your hands will be positioned above your elbows. At the same time bend your knees to lower your center of gravity which also helps you get the paddle at a lower angle.

The active phase is bracing or slapping the blade's powerface against the water. This creates resistance, particularly if the blade is relatively flat to the water. At the moment your blade makes contact, creating resistance, try and shift your weight towards your left leg. Between this and the blade bracing against the water hopefully you'll regain your balance.

The Low Brace: This is really just another bracing option but instead of bracing with the powerface you brace with the backface. The dynamics are the same in terms of protecting your shoulders by keeping your elbows close to your torso and shifting the paddle to a low angle relative to the water. As the name implies the paddle

Low Brace with backface of blade facing downward

Bow Draw

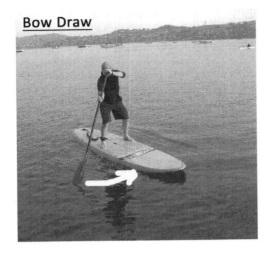

is held lower to the water meaning your hands move to a position below your elbows.

I encourage you to play with these two types of braces. Depending on where your paddle is positioned and conditions you find yourself in, you'll find that one or the other feels more natural and effective.

Bow and stern draw: These strokes have some similarities with some of the other strokes we've discussed and are also used to adjust or control the direction of the nose or tail of your SUP. A simple bow draw stroke starts off with reaching your paddle forward

Stern Draw

as far as your normal catch position. Two differences though. First, in that forward position you now extend your paddle out further and then hit the catch with your powerface parallel to the nose as you draw it to the rail. If you do this on the right side it will swing your nose to the right. You can also change the angle of the powerface

as it draws towards the nose's rail. Turn the inside edge of the powerface towards the rail setting a 35-45 degree angle. You'll find this easier to do.

When would you use a bow draw? You could simply be at a

standstill where you want to turn the nose of your SUP one way or the other. Also paddlers often incorporate the bow draw into the forward stroke which in effect would be similar to the beginning of the C-stroke without the last part where the paddle completes the bottom of the C.

The stern draw: Reach back and out with the powerface parallel and facing the rear rail and then pull it towards the stern. Again, as in the bow draw you can also play with the angles.

The Sculling bow/nose draw: This stroke shares some of the attributes of the sculling brace but is used to pivot the nose of your SUP in one direction. This is a fun stroke when you are at a standstill and wish to turn the nose of your board. Yes you can use your cross bow sweep or regular sweep strokes to achieve the same thing. But simply put this is a fun stroke that is also effective.

Initiate this stroke by reaching your paddle out as far as possible to the side of your hips. Plant the blade in the water with the powerface oriented forward. Now sweep the paddle forward and arc it towards the nose of your SUP powered by your torso rotation.

Blade should be fully submerged for the entire stroke

As you complete the arc let the powerface turn towards the rail so that at the end of this stroke the powerface will be facing the rail. Now recover your paddle to the initial catch position by your side by slicing it back through the water and repeat as needed. Keep the blade submerged the entire time.

You can take the same concept and throw it in reverse for a **sculling stern/tail draw**. In this case plant your paddle off your board adjacent to your hips with the powerface in normal position. Now using torso rotation draw the paddle backwards and then arc it towards the tail. Let the powerface turn as the paddle arcs with the powerface ending up facing the rear rail. Recover by slicing the blade through the water to the start position.

Just as in the sculling brace strokes you can change the angle of the paddle shaft relative to the water. A lower angle and you'll combine bracing with pivoting the nose or tail. A high angle and you'll have more turning power.

Slicing draw stroke: This is a stroke that can move your SUP sideways but one that is not often used. There are also other styles of draw strokes for moving your board sideways but I'll just describe this one.

Rotate your torso towards the paddle while reaching your paddle as far as you can opposite your hip position. Plant the blade in the water with the powerface parallel to your SUP. Try and keep the paddle shaft vertical while pulling the paddle close but not all the way to the edge of the SUP. Remember, to help keep the paddle shaft vertical for a more powerful stroke you'll need to position your top hand just past the rail or edge of the board. Now recover back to the catch position by slicing the blade back out. As the blade slices back to the catch position you should be seeing the powerface side and not the backface. Need more stability, drop the top hand but your sideways movement will not be as powerful.

Admittedly this is not the most efficient stroke in our SUP inventory. You'll also find it challenging to move your SUP sideways

From Catch position pull towards rail

Slicing Draw Stroke

Slice blade back out to catch position. Remember, blade remains fully sub-merged for the entire stroke.

Slicing Draw Stroke

without either the nose or tail swinging. One way to deal with swing is to change the catch position. If you are executing a draw stroke on the right side and you find the tail swings in that direction you can shift your catch position forward and this draws the nose to the right and hence counteracts your tail swing in that direction.

More Advanced Stuff

Unstacked Shoulders

Stacked Shoulders

Stacking the shoulders: World renowned surfer and SUP paddler Dave Kalama talks about stacking the shoulders as part of a powerful forward stroke. Remember that the top hand is positioned over the lower hand to achieve a more vertical and hence efficient stroke. You can actually achieve this by keeping your shoulders fairly level but a better way for more power is to *stack* your shoulders. Therefore in conjunction with the forward crunch/rotation, bend your torso a little to the side (towards the paddle). This will stack or raise your left shoulder above your right shoulder (assuming your paddling on the right). This gives you more energy transfer from your torso through your arms to the paddle.

Paddle placement at the catch: In general, during the forward stroke we talked about the blade coming alongside the rail starting at the catch and moving straight backwards to the exit. We can fine tune this a bit. In reality, SUP rails are curved and not even widths at every point along the length. In perfect conditions, for a SUP board to move forward in a straight manner, you plant the blade and draw it straight back. Well if you plant your blade at the catch against your SUPs rail, and it remains against the rail for the entire stroke it is actually following the curvature or arc of the side of the board right? After all, the mid-point of the board is wider than the forward section where the catch begins. Therefore the blade is not traveling straight back or as the pros say the blade is not pulling the board straight forward.

So stab your blade in at the catch just off the rail (6-8 inches) and by the time it travels back to your hips it should be gracing the rail. This will help you achieve a straighter paddling path.

Pivot Turn: This is a fun one but also a good way to get wet. The idea behind this stroke is to submerge the tail and pivot the board for a quick turn. Consider that you have a centerline that runs down the middle of your SUP. Now you're going to shift from your normal side by side foot stance to a surfer stance. Drop your right foot back so your heal hits the centerline and your right foot is at a 45 degree angle to this line. Your left foot remains in front but with the left toes gracing the centerline. This foot is also at about a 45 degree angle. As you get more comfortable you'll work your way further back until you start sinking the tail. You'll find the sweet spot where the tail is sinking and the nose is lifting without flipping backwards. Now sweep the paddle on one side and watch the board turn quickly. If this doesn't happen you're probably already in the water. You can continue sweeping your paddle around the tail of your board to the other side.

To add to the challenge try a reverse sweep. To lessen the challenge start off in a seated or kneeling position to get a feel for balance as you work your way back towards the tail.

Sculling Brace: A sculling brace is a very supportive type of brace. You might use this type of brace; if for example, you have stopped paddling and the waters bumpy enough you need some support. A sculling brace is a fluid brace where the paddle sculls forward and backwards in the water more or less in a figure eight pattern. The angle of the blade is very important here as is the relative angle of the paddle shaft to the water's surface.

First of all rotate your torso towards the side your paddle is on. To get started reach your paddle a couple feet in front of you. Just like in bracing drop your top hand down to achieve a low angle

Pivot Turn

Pivot Turn

Paddle Strokes & Getting Started

49

between the paddle shaft and water. Now as you scull the paddle back tilt the powerface so it's traveling through the water at about a 35-45 degree angle (meaning the outside edge of the powerface gets tilted towards the rail). Once you reach a couple feet behind you tilt the powerface to face forward at a 35-45 degree angle (meaning the inside edge gets titled outward) and sweep forward. As you do this back and forth motion the paddle blade will travel along a small arc. You can further experiment by making the sculling path shorter or longer, by increasing the degree you tilt the powerface and by moving your top hand up in the air more or down further. By playing with these variables you'll feel varying degrees of support, resistance and efficiency.

Hawaiian vs. Tahitian Forward Paddling Stroke: These are the two main styles of paddling. Around where I paddle the Hawaiian style is typical. But here are some of the differences as I understand it. The Hawaiian paddle stroke is a more powerful and longer stroke but also in some ways less energy efficient. At the exit you typically drop the top hand downwards to the side as the blade slices out of the water. Then as you are reaching for the catch the top hand swings back up until it's vertically aligned above the lower hand just as you hit the catch. The stroke ends at your ankles.

In contrast, the Tahitian paddle stroke is executed at a faster cadence and the stroke length is a bit shorter ending before or by your toes. Also, the blade exits the water not by slicing it outwards but by lifting the blade directly upwards. The analogy, expert paddler Dave Kalama uses is that it's like pulling a sword out of its scabbard. Now once the blade exits the water rotate the top hand and thumb forward so the blade cuts through the air until it reaches the catch position. Unlike in the Hawaiian style the top hand does not drop down very much as you exit, feather the blade and initiate the recovery phase. So higher cadence, choppier shorter strokes and a different exit and recovery technique. Racers who paddle Tahitian style maintain a very high stroke rate that would put most weekend warriors into cardiac arrest. But these guys are in incredible shape.

Getting Started

In this section we'll discuss some basic strategies for getting started on the water. I'll make the assumption that you have chosen a calm body of water and the wind is minimal because these are the best conditions for your initial SUP experiences. Maybe you are renting a board from an outfitter. You can expect for them to give you some immediate guidelines in terms of basic strokes and local safety concerns.

I'm also assuming you are dressed for the local conditions whether it is a wetsuit day or not and that you have your PFD with you. First off, carry your board to the edge of the water and wrap your leash around your ankle. Remember, this valuable piece of gear is going to keep you from getting separated from your board if you fall off. Next bring your board into deep enough water so that the fin doesn't drag on the bottom.

Safety position: You should start off in what I call the basic safety position. This means getting on your board on your knees instead of starting off standing on your feet. Why bother? It is critical for you to be comfortable in going from a kneeling position to a standing position and back again. If you get caught in increasing winds, choppy waters or get hit by a boat wake and find yourself off balance or falling into the water repeatedly you need to get down into your safety position. The kneeling position achieves a number of results quickly. Firstly, it lowers your center of gravity and gives you much greater balance. Secondly, you've just reduced the size of your body's natural sail which loves to catch the wind when you are standing upright. And finally with better balance and a smaller wind profile, the kneeling position is a powerful position from where you can make forward progress on those windy and choppy days.

So position your knees on both sides of the mid-point or carrying handle of your SUP. Start off by tilting the board side to side to

get a feel for the board's tippy factor. Obviously, if you can't even paddle the SUP while on your knees you probably need a more stable board. Now paddle around close to shore and practice all your basic strokes. Work on your forward and sweep strokes, the reverse sweep and stopping and backing up. As you practice try and incorporate all the paddling stroke concepts I discussed in the various paddling stroke sections. Remember to use your torso to power your strokes.

A quick tip. A lot of paddlers find it awkward to hold the paddle in the normal hand position (spread apart ninety degrees with the top hand on the hand grip) while on their knees since you're much closer to the water. For most people it easier to choke down on the paddle meaning that you put your top hand also on the paddle shaft. Let's say your paddling on the right side. Your lower hand would be your right hand in its normal position. But both hands should be positioned on the paddle shaft with thumbs up and therefore your top hand knuckles would be facing the board. So in effect, the palms of your hands are facing one another, and from an ergonomic standpoint this reduces stress on the top hand wrist.

Also while working on your strokes and getting more comfortable on the board in the kneeling position throw in a few short sprints with a powerful forward stroke. This is just to tune you up in case you get caught out in the wind so you have a little feeling for what it takes to power up.

Standing up: Now you're ready to stand up. Get the board moving with some power strokes. A moving board is more stable. Face forward and hold your paddle in one hand either at your side, parallel to the SUPs centerline or across the board in front of your knees. Do your best to keep the board balanced with weight on both sides. Now slide one foot forward so it's in line with your other knee. Next push down on your hands, steadying your board and bring your other foot forward and immediately move into a standing position. A fellow paddler uses the

expression *stand up, look up* because as he says the brain needs the horizon to balance. As soon as you can, start paddling, because this will give you more stability. Paddle around for a while and get used to the balance of your SUP. As you get more comfortable you should review all your basic strokes.

Finally, it's a smart idea to practice going back to your safety position and then again back to a stand up position until this becomes comfortable. You never know when you might need it.

At this point, if you haven't fallen in repeatedly and you feel a basic level of confidence that you can control your board, it's time to go for a paddle. If you can follow the shoreline or let's say a series of marinas this is a good idea in case conditions change and you need to get to the shore or a dock quickly. Keep the offshore paddling for a later date until you've achieved a certain mastery of all your basic paddling strokes, and have had a little experience with falling off your board and climbing back on. And you should have that kneeling to standing thing down pat. With time you'll eventually develop the comfort and ability to deal with moderate to stronger winds, wind chop and small swells. And then the funs really going to begin.

Tripod

A note on foot position. If you find your feet out of position, one way to move on the board for a beginner is by hopping forward or backward. With this technique you can avoid lifting one foot at a time where your other foot takes all your weight and tips your SUP over. So get comfortable with hopping back and forth on your board by practicing in shallow water or by the shoreline. A more conservative approach is *called the **Tripod**. Here you plant the paddle in front of you on the center of the board. Put weight on the paddle to stabilize as you shift your feet to the necessary position.*

Launching Scenarios: Again I'm just going to talk about calm condition environments. The easiest place to launch from is a sandy beach by the lake or bay when there's no wind or waves. But what if it's a rocky beach and the water beyond beckons? The main difference is that you're going to want to have some good foot protection to clamber over the rocks on shore, and that also might be in the water. In this situation you simply have to make sure your board, and importantly your skeg, are in deep enough water so they don't get dinged up.

A little more difficult challenge is an off the dock launch. Standing at the edge of the dock slide your board through your hands until the nose hits the water. Now lower the tail into the water. If the water surface is close to the docks top deck edge you can do this

with your hands and kneeling or bending over. If there's a decent drop you can lower the tail by holding the leash. If not already now put your leash on. Sit your butt on the edge of the dock and place both feet on the board near the balance point.

With weight on your dockside hand get yourself into a kneeling position. Always leave or approach a dock on your knees to avoid the possibility of losing your balance and hitting the dock. A firm grip on the dock should ensure that your board doesn't suddenly slip away from the dock. When ready you can either give a slight push to move away from the dock or use a draw stroke to do the same.

*As a beginner it's not unsual to develop **foot cramps** from gripping the board to avoid falling over. One instructor I know recommends flopping into the water from your board to get over this innate fear. Besides this, wiggle your toes, and lifting one foot up at a time rotate your feet in circles. Finally, spread your body's weight evenly between the front and back of your feet.*

There are many other possible launching scenarios of course. Let's say you're in the Caribbean sailing island to island. First off, thank your lucky stars for being in a beautiful paradise, but more so for the fact that there's a SUP onboard. But the water's a big drop from the deck. No problem. The turquoise waters are crystal clear; you can see angel fish swimming casually about and no rocks in sight. Toss the board over the rail and jump in yourself. Slither up the board like mounting a surfboard. Attach your leash, go from kneel to standing position and off you go. One note, if you jump with your paddle in hand rather then throw it in the water make sure and position it so it won't bonk you in the face when you hit the water.

What's SUP?

Chapter 3   Safety On The Water

The emphasis of this chapter is to get you focused on having a safe experience while paddling, and to give you tools to deal with challenging scenarios that just might happen. Let's face it you're reading this book because you're seeking adventure. And with adventure there is exposure and risk. But what most of us want is calculated risk, controlled by proper preparation, awareness of the variables, and skills to deal with situations that inevitably come up.

That said, be realistic about your personal fitness level. This includes your abilities as a swimmer and your comfort level in the water, both good things to be proficient at. In general, the buddy system in most outdoor activities is a good idea but there is a counter argument to this. There is a point where your "buddy" can put the two of you at risk if their abilities relative to the conditions are seriously lacking. For example, trying to rescue someone in conditions that you can barely handle will put you both in jeopardy. Regardless, if you go solo let someone know your *flight plan*. Where and how long you are going.

Weather conditions

It's a typical piece of advice for you to check in on weather conditions for the area where you'll be paddling. Sounds simplistic but it's surprising how many people don't do this when there's so much information easily accessed. You might as well know what the predictions are. Is there a forecast for the winds to pick up? And what time of day? Get on the water early before the wind comes. There's lots of resources online and with a little patience and even advice from the local kayak, paddleboard and or surf shop you can tune into the best weather sites. You can get wind, swell and current reports all online. At marine stores you can pick up a tidelog if you're in an area affected by tides and currents (also online).

A classic question is what level of wind can I paddle in? What kind of currents can I handle? What kind of choppy conditions can I handle? It is not within the context of this book to answer these questions as there are so many variables mostly dealing with your own abilities. But let me repeat what I said earlier. As a beginner you want to seek out calm conditions: meaning no wind to a light breeze at most, minimal currents, no chop or swell patterns and limited boat traffic. With time, as your skills and fitness levels increase, you'll develop an understanding of the differing conditions under which you are comfortable paddling in. You'll also begin to figure out what it means to paddle in a 5mph wind versus 10mph so you can relate this experience to weather reports and whether or not you should go out in the first place.

Keep in mind there's what the weather report tells you and there's what is really going on at the specific location you're paddling from. The point is that ultimately the determining factor in going out or not is what you find once at the location. This neatly segues into getting to know the local weather patterns which can be different than the general reports you read online or not!

A couple tips that might be obvious to you.   If it's windy, if possible, pick a route upwind first and take the downwind run home. If the wind is blowing offshore stick close to the shoreline. Are currents an issue in your area? Often current cycles last for hours. So if you are just going out for an hour maybe paddle first against the current and then use it to come home.

Safety Equipment

Your first line of safety is making appropriate decisions about the conditions and whether or not to go out. Next is having basic safety gear with you and of course the list can be short or as long as you want. There's always new stuff to be purchased for those gearheads in the group.

In the clothing section I already talked about the intelligence of dressing for the conditions and the possibility of immersion. So we'll move on from here. A SUP is defined as a "vessel" by the US Coast Guard and this is one reason a personal flotation device is required. (The most popular is a Coast Guard approved Type III PFD. Type I & II offer more buoyancy but being bulkier are not the industry standard.) The other reason is simply good common sense for your own protection. The exceptions to this rule according to the Coast Guard are in the surf or designated swim areas where PFDs are not required. (More on this in the surf section.) Also, with the designation as a vessel a "sound producing device, navigational lights and accident reporting are required."

For a sound producing device to get attention a whistle is acceptable, and it's probably best to attach it to your PFD. Navigational lights? The standard red and green lights that sail and powerboats use are not required. You just need to have a flashlight starting at dusk to alert other boats to your position. As for an accident report, this is usually required if there is a death, an injury beyond First Aid, a missing person or a certain amount of property damage. The exact requirements vary from state to state and the report must be filed with the relative state authority. For example, in California that would be the California Department of Boating and Waterways. You know, you rammed into a sailboat and it sunk. Better report this.

One final attempt to get you to wear your PFD instead of placing it somewhere on your board. If you are injured, semi-conscious or unconscious the PFD is not going to do you any good unless it's on. If you forgot your leash or haven't yet purchased one and you get separated from your board and are getting tired it's good to have it on you. Waving at it while your board drifts off might be good for your sense of humor but not for saving your life.

From here the **list of gear** you might bring with you can get extensive and depends on the paddling conditions, your abilities and the length of your excursion.

Marine VHF radio: Simply put it's a smart personal safety device to have along. A VHF (very high frequency) radio will give you the ability to send out a distress signal if you or someone else is in trouble, and also allow you to contact other vessels on the water including the Coast Guard for assistance. It's a great investment. Get a waterproof one. Channel

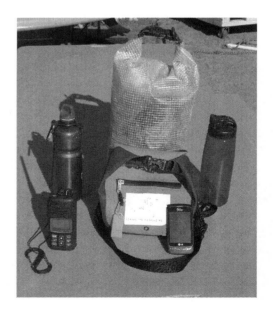

16 is used as the emergency channel on a VHF radio for distress calls. Other channels can be chosen to communicate with anyone on the water, including your friends if they also have a radio.

A cheaper or interim solution to this is to use your cell phone. A call to 911 can be patched over to the Coast Guard. Besides this, you can let your honey know when to have dinner ready.

Waterproof fanny pack: This gives you waterproof storage for some energy bars, your cell phone, sunscreen and other choice items. You can also hook your VHF radio onto the waist band.

Tow rope: I'll discuss tow ropes and towing later in the towing scenarios section. But here are a couple thoughts. If you are paddling with others, especially if they are more inexperienced or are young kids a tow rope is great thing to have. If the wind picks up and your fellow paddler is struggling in the wind you can assist them with your tow rope.

Hydration: Always a good idea but how to carry it is the question? Options: You can wear a Camelback type of hydration system or maybe your fanny pack has a drink holder. If you have deck rigging tuck a bottle under this. The ultimate might be a deck mounted H2O holder.

A drybag and extra layers etc.: I'm focusing here mostly on day trips and situations where weather conditions might change over time. Camping and SUPing is another subject that I'm not going to get into. Let's say you paddle a couple miles, crossing over from the shoreline to an island. You decide to stop on the island and have lunch. Clouds roll over and the

air temperature falls and you start getting chilled. You dig into your drybag and voila you've got some warm clothes and your lunch. Or maybe you pull out a wetsuit for the return trip because the water's getting choppy and you want protection against possible immersion. The drybag would have been stashed under the deck rigging on your SUP. If your SUP doesn't come with anyway to strap on a drybag you can buy kits for this purpose.

Self-rescues and safety positions

In this section I'll talk about things related to self-rescues. One of the first things you need to know is how to fall. Assuming you've lost your balance you definitely don't want to bonk your head on the edge of your board or hit some submerged object. A fellow SUP instructor coaches his students to fall into the water in "starfish" position. In other words arms and legs spread out and fall flat on the water. The point is not to dive in head or feet first were you could potentially hit something. Maybe another way to describe this is to do a belly or back flop because after all scientists no longer call them starfish but instead sea stars (since they aren't related to fish).

I know you probably don't want to do this but as a beginner it's a good idea to practice falling off your board and getting back on. There are several ways to mount your board. One way is to approach your board at the mid-point with your chest at about a 45 degree angle to the rail. Place your hands on opposite sides of

the board as best you can, kick with your legs while pulling yourself up onto the board. An option to this, which some find easier, is to start back at the tail and slide the board under your chest and pull yourself up to the mid-point.

Once onboard get into your safety position and start paddling or if comfortable move to a standing position. If you remain in your safety position on your knees you also have the option to drop your butt on top of your heels which further lowers your center of gravity and takes the pressure off your knees.

Finally, if you're still at risk of tipping over while in the kneeling/ sitting position lie prone on your board. This is the most stable position you can be in but of course you can't use your paddle and using your arms means moving a lot slower. Position your paddle so it is secure and out of the way. This means lining the paddle up with the centerline with the blade just under the top of your chest and the handle reaching towards the nose of the SUP.

Lost your paddle? If you're in the water get on your board first, especially if you're not wearing a leash. The wind will carry your board away a lot faster than the paddle. Once on your board remain in a prone position and like a surfer paddle to retrieve your paddle. If for some reason you can't get to your paddle it's better to be on your board anyway. At least now you are out of the water and less likely to get hypothermic, and you are more visible to anyone who might assist you. Plus paddling your board surfer style is faster than swimming to get to safety and warmth.

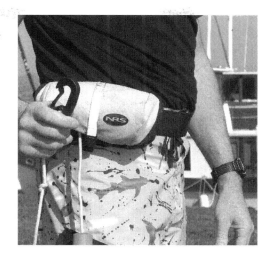

Towing scenarios and assisting others: First off, if things get bad and you have that VHF radio or cell phone call for help. Or try and flag down a boater. But a lot of times there's no immediate danger and you just need to assist your fellow paddler.

I mentioned carrying a tow rope as a piece of safety gear earlier. Personally I think the best tow system is one where you have a waist belt tow rope with a quick release. The quick release allows you to jettison your tow rope in case of a situation like entanglement. And the waist type system provides easy access since you're wearing it. The question of how to actually tow the person you're helping has many answers.

Towing from the nose: This is ideal. If you are assisting someone who can still paddle either in a standing or kneeling position attach your tow rope to a leash plug on the front deck of their SUP. However, most boards don't come with a leash plug on the front forward

deck. (It would be a good idea for manufacturers to start adding a factory install attachment point for towing scenarios.) You can buy an aftermarket leash plug and install it yourself. You'd need to add on a small loop of strong line to which you attach/clip-on the tow rope.

Towing from the deck rigging: Some SUPs come with deck rigging running through inset plugs or glued on mounts for holding down a drybag, water bottle etc. The deck rigging is normally positioned near the front of the board so this could be another attachment point for your tow rope.

Tow rope held by the paddler: This can work if there's no practical tow rope attachment point. Have your paddler sit or lie prone while holding the tow rope. Depending on how they are oriented they obviously have to make sure to hold onto their paddle. One approach is to put the tip of the paddle blade under their butt or chest with the handle towards the nose of the SUP. Yet another option is to wrap the tow rope around their paddler's paddle shaft at about mid-point. One of their hands will secure this connection, and the other will

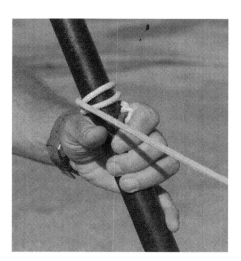

grip the shaft lower down. Now the paddler can be towed while also using their paddle to help keep their board going straight forward.

What if you don't have a tow rope? The best option here is to use your leash. Take it off your ankle and secure it to the leash plug on the nose of the rescue's deck. No leash plug? Then the next option is any deck rigging they have up front otherwise they'll have to hold onto it whether sitting or lying prone as in the above example.

You'll hear about other scenarios. You don't have a leash but your friend does and they need help in the strong headwind. Although it's been suggested that you can tow them using their leash with their tail facing forward this is a very ineffective way to move through the water. Having the skeg at the front creates all kinds of problems related to drag and the board going this way and that. Some say to then remove the skeg from this board. Really you have all this time to tinker around? I doubt it. In this scenario it would be more effective to take their leash off and attach it to your leash plug and then tow them as they hold the other end with their SUP facing nose first. If your board doesn't have a leash plug then wear the leash and hand the person you're helping the other end.

Besides dealing with wind issues there are other reasons why you might need to assist another paddler and of course equally as many ways to do this. I'll just give you a few ideas. Let's say you are out with someone who is more a novice than you are and they seem to have some genetic predisposition to vertigo. They simply can't stay upright on their board, and taking it one step further they no longer have the energy or ability to crawl back up on their board. There are several ways you can help. One approach is to parallel park your SUP next to their board. Keeping weight on your board reach over and help pull them onto their board. Another approach is to go to the nose of their board while directing them to the tail of their board. Position your board perpendicular to their SUPs nose. In a seated or kneeling position lift the nose of their board in order to sink the tail. Have them reach up as far as they can on the rails of

their board and pull themselves up as if sliding up onto a surfboard while you push the nose down. Once you get them back on board you can start towing.

Of course this all sounds great in calm water. Imagine the challenge in wind and chop! Therefore it's important to practice a variety of scenarios in different conditions if you want to learn what it takes to assist other paddlers.

How about something easier? Sometimes it's just a matter of

stabilizing your partners board to give them a rest and so that you can communicate. This is an easy one. Paddle up to the nose of their board, in perpendicular position and go to a kneeling position. Lift the nose part way across the mid-section of your board. Now you have a stable raft. You can sit and have a chat, share food or come up with a game plan if needed.

Paddling in challenging headwind conditions: Assuming you are starting out in relatively calm bodies of water one of the most challenging things you're likely to face is an increase in wind speed. We've already talked about dropping to your safety position if necessary. However, if you are still comfortable standing there are several approaches to tackling strong winds.

One is using what's called a ***choke stroke.*** The wind is picking up and it's slowing down your forward movement. Drop your top hand just below the handle, forefinger and thumb around the neck of the handle where it meets the top of the paddle shaft. Continue to paddle aggressively, fully immersing your paddle blade. You are beginning to lower your bodies *sail* to create less wind resistance. Now choke down further as you paddle on. The idea is that the choke stroke is a progressive stroke where you keep choking downward, as needed, and hence progressively reduce your profile

Choke Stroke
Start by choking down on shaft and lowering body profile

Progressively lower body and choke down as needed

Dropping down to the board

If needed drop to safety position on knees

to the wind. The key is to fully immerse your blade with each stroke which forces you to crunch down. Eventually you'll find yourself on your knees if necessary.

Another approach to dealing with strong winds relates to the problem you'll encounter in keeping your board traveling in a straight direction. Potentially the wind and chop will constantly push your board off course either to the right or left. Let's take an example where you are heading upwind (into the wind) but conditions keep pushing you to the right. Even a skilled paddler will have a challenge in this scenario but a good way to deal with this is by combining strokes. When paddling on the right side you'll use mostly forward sweep strokes to help steer the nose back to the left. In conjunction with the sweep strokes you can shift more weight onto your right rail which will also help you correct your board to the left. Finally, when you switch sides and paddle on the left side, initiate your forward stroke with a bow draw to pull the nose left and then transition into your forward stroke. You can also try a C or J stroke on the left side as another way to pull the board to the left but these are more challenging strokes in such dynamic conditions.

Basically you have to experiment with combining strokes when necessary to control the direction of your board in strong winds and chop.

If the level of wind is too intense to use the above techniques effectively you can try tacking. With tacking you'll paddle with the wind coming at you at a 45 degree angle one way then turn and go the other way using the same angle. In effect you are zigzagging upwind to your final destination.

Paddling in choppy conditions: Ocean swell or bay chop, or boat wakes coming at you from the side or beam makes it more likely you'll flip off your board. If you are faced with this situation the best technique is to paddle directly into any chop coming your way. If you can, drop one foot back a bit to raise the nose of your

Tacking in wind &
chop at a 45% angle

wind & chop direction

Drop one foot back
to raise the nose and
power over the chop

board over the wave and drive the board forward with your paddle strokes. Then return back to a parallel stance, switching back and forth as needed.

The classic problem is where you are spearing through the chop to maintain stability but this is not taking you in the direction you need to get to shore. If you need to move to the right or left, taking the chop at a 45 degree angle will still give you lots of stability while allowing you to move sideways in the direction you need. Of course, you can vary the angle depending on comfort. We'll discuss more scenarios in terms of surf conditions in the chapter on surfing.

Another thing you might need to do for stability is to lower the angle of your strokes. So instead of a vertical forward stroke, drop your top hand down, bend your knees more and overall you'll lower your center of gravity and become more stable. Taking this further you can execute wider strokes and even change the angle of the blade through the water by tilting the outside edge of the paddle towards the board. This will enhance stability but lower your board speed. So now you'll have a low wider stroke with the blade angled which will offer some bracing with each stroke.

Fin Placement: Your SUP fin can play a critical role in how your board handles in different conditions. If for example, you are paddling into the wind and it's challenging to keep your SUP from being pushed off course or blown sideways, then turning power is obviously critical. Besides combining strokes, as I mentioned earlier in this section, you can move your fin forward. Your board will respond to your turning strokes easier than if the fin is centered or pushed back in the fin slot. Obviously you would have to anticipate the need to move your fin before commencing your paddle.

On the other hand if you were doing a downwind run or simply looking for your board to track straight you'd want to slide the fin back in the slot.

There are also the other variables of fin size and shape. For example, a racer doing a downwind course would want a longer and straighter fin (perhaps up to 15") for tracking purposes. A shorter curved fin on the other hand would be better for a course that involved lots of turns.

Remember, when in doubt always keep your paddle active. The

pressure of the paddle against the water and any forward movement will give you more stability then having your paddle out of the water. In reality you'll end up combining all these different approaches to dealing with wind and chop to get where you need to go. Ultimately, if you find the conditions are way over your head, and you keep falling off your board, get into the prone position to maintain stability. You'll lose body heat faster if you're spending lots of time in the water than if you're lying on your board.

Paddle & Board
An awesome view & workout

Chapter 4   SUP Fitness Exercises

There are many ways to enjoy the experience of being on the water on a SUP while getting fit. There's the catch-all category of *fitness exercises* which covers a broad range of activities.

For example, you can transfer many land based exercises to the floating platform, working the major muscle groups with push-ups, sit-ups and squats. We call this **SUP Fitness Exercises**.

Then there's **SUP Yoga**. With the popularity of yoga these days it's not surprising that students of this ancient art are finding their inner calm on a SUP board.

Finally, **SUP Fitness Paddling** includes doing short and long intervals. An extension of this is racing for those of you who want to take SUP fitness to a higher level, challenge yourself and make new friends on the racing circuit.

Of course, there's no reason you can't combine all of these fitness approaches together creating your own unique workout. What's most important is that you learn proper technique and pace yourself when trying new exercises. Again a few lessons with experts will accelerate the learning curve along with the abundance of written and online materials you can find. Classes with qualified experts will also ensure good form and protect against injuries.

All of these SUP fitness approaches will **develop your core**. I talked about the core in my introduction. I could lay the scientific definitions and esoteric muscles groups on you, but in layman's language the core covers muscles from your lower neck to just above your knees. Most people actually just say your torso but let's not quibble. These muscles control the movement of your mid-body in stabilizing it while we do the things we love like paddling, tennis, volleyball, running etc. Specifically, the core muscles contract and stabilize the shoulders, spine and the pelvic region.

Some of these well-known muscles are upper back and shoulders, lower back, abdominals, butt muscles and hip flexors. If all the muscles are working in a healthy and efficient manner they give you the power and efficiency to move through your sporting world.

Here's an analogy I read and like. Your core muscles (torso) are like the foundation of a house. You can have a strong foundation or a weak foundation and it affects everything around it. And that's why if it's good for the core it's great for building a solid foundation to enjoy all those activities you like.

Let's start out with a few stretching exercises which you can choose to include before and or after any of the fitness exercises I discuss in this chapter. Refer to the photos for positioning.

Start off with the ***shoulder opening stretch***. Since you engage your shoulders so much when paddling this is a good one. Next do

Shoulder Opening Stretch

a *low back stretch* and let your butt sink downward, stretching the lower back. From this position sit down with your legs extended in front of you. You can do several hamstring stretches. One would be simply reaching forward and grasping your feet. Try and stretch forward from your hips and not your back. You'll feel your hamstrings lengthening. From here you can go into a *cross hamstring stretch*.

Low Back Stretch

Cross Hamstring Stretch

Next try an ***outer hip/torso opening stretch*** and then finish up by turning on your belly and doing a ***thigh stretch***.

SUP Fitness Exercises

As you can imagine the long list of resistance exercise you can do on a SUP is endless but we'll stick to the more popular ones. Before you get started warm up with a five minute paddle just to get the juices flowing. Now do your best to find calm water away from any distractions.

At some future date you might purchase a small anchor at a marine shop and secure it with line to your SUP so you don't drift. Another consideration is what to do with your paddle. If you have deck rigging you could tuck the blade or handle under this and let the rest of the paddle dangle in the water. Or you wrap your leash around the paddle shaft instead of your ankle and let it drift.

You're going to aim for 10-15 reps of each exercise and three sets with a short 1-2 minute break in-between.

Push-ups: Lie prone on your board and position your hands in line with your shoulders but a bit wider. As you do your push-ups make sure and keep your back straight and don't raise your butt. Push-up to full extension then lower yourself back down without touching the board and repeat. If you find this too hard you can cheat by leaving your knees on the board. This exercise will primarily

work your chest and arm muscles but since you are on an unstable platform it will also work some of your finer core muscles as they work to stabilize your body.

Abdominal Crunches

Abdominal crunches: Back flat against the board, knees bent with hands clasped behind your head. Now crunch your body forward focusing on contracting your stomach muscles. You can do three sets of these and then do the same again but this time twist your torso as you crunch forward. First to the right and then the left and back and forth.

Knee to chest: This will also work the abdominals. Remain on your back with knees bent and your hands at your sides with palms

Knees to Chest

Bridge

flat against the board. Now lift your knees back to your chest and repeat.

Bridge: Here's a couple variations to work the stomach muscles and strengthen the lower back. Again back against the board. Knees bent with your heels of your feet about a foot in front of your butt. Now bridge your lower back up in the air, hold it a second, release and then repeat. You can make this a little more challenging and do a single leg bridge. Extend one leg straight out parallel to the board and then lift your butt and lower back off the board into bridge position. Do all the reps with the same leg extended and

Plank

True Plank

then switch.

Plank: This exercise strengthens the body and elongates the spine. Rotate into a prone position. Put your forearms flat on the board with the elbows positioned under your shoulders. The palms of your hands are pressed against the deck. Curl your toes forward and now raise your body off the board keeping your legs straight and your butt down (looking like a straight plank). Hold for 30 seconds, relax and then repeat two more times. From this initial plank position you can go into what is called *True Plank* position where you raise your body up on your extended arms (position hands under shoulders). This is similar to a push up. Maintain breathing and let your elbows bend slightly and hold for 30 seconds then repeat a few times.

Tricep Dips

Tricep dips: It's hard to get the full range here but start by sitting on your butt with your legs extended in front of you. Place your hands on each side, palms flat on the board, fingers facing forward. Hand placement would be about ½ foot behind your butt. Now lift your butt and knees up. You can start off by sliding your feet towards your knees as you bend the knees. Hold your butt up as high as you can and lower and raise yourself via your arms. Focus on working the tricep muscle. As you get better with this movement stretch your legs out more keeping your legs straight and your butt up. This will throw more weight onto your triceps as you dip up and down.

SUP Yoga

You can bring your land based yoga practice onto the water or start on your SUP for the first time. The challenge offered by the SUP over the yoga matt is that it is a more unstable platform. This in turn can work some of those finer core and stabilizer muscles. Most people find this adds to their practice besides the connection to being out in nature. Below I'll share a series of basic yoga poses for you to get started.

Yoga is a tradition that began in India more than three thousand years ago and the intention is to develop a healthy mind, body and spirit. Specifically the word yoga, from the ancient Indian language **Sanskrit***, means the union of mind and spirit. Yoga poses are called* **asanas***.*

For those new to yoga the concern is "how will I remember these poses on the water without this book?" Easy enough, just practice the listed series of poses at home on a matt or rug first. Then you can write up a short "cheat sheet" listing the poses and bring this with you.

First off, do an easy warm-up paddle and some stretching. Now find a calm location and let's get started. Just sit on your board for a couple minutes and start with some breathing exercises. Bring the breath in deep and exhale. Work towards feeling more relaxed, imagining tension flowing out of your body as you exhale. Mix it up by breathing through one nostril several times then the other. Always keep in mind your position on the board in terms of balance so move slowly!

Seated Prayer pose: Sit on your board and cross your legs if

Seated Prayer Pose

you can. If not extend your legs in front with knees bent and heels making contact with the board. Now place your hands together in prayer position and push your chest up and forward. In conjunction with this lift your shoulders and pull them outward and back. Now turn your face skyward. As part of this pose you want to maintain your lumbar curve so don't slump, and feel like you're stretching your spine. Now let your body relax then repeat the pose 6 times.

This pose benefits your lower back, neck and shoulders and helps get you centered.

Child's pose: This is a relaxing pose. Sit with your knees bent underneath you with your butt resting on the top of your heels. The top of your feet will be pressed against the board deck with toes pointing backwards. Drop your chest down, stomach resting on your thighs and forehead touching the board. Position your arms stretched out in front of you, palms of hands against the deck. Now breathe and relax.

Child's Pose

Child's pose stretches the hips, thighs and ankles. Not a good pose if you have a knee injury.

Table Top pose: From Child's pose move into position on your

Table Top
Pose

Table Top Pose
Arched Back

hands and knees. The palms of your hands should be directly below your shoulders with your fingers spread out. Your knees are hip-width apart, positioned below the hips with your toes pointed backwards. Look forward lengthening your neck.

Hold this asana for about 5 breaths. In between holding this asana you can mix it up by looking downward and arching your back then lowering your belly. Repeat this sequence about 6-10 times.

This pose is a foundation pose that leads to many other poses

Sunbird Pose

but also helps align the spine and head.

Sunbird pose: This is a fun one that will also challenge your balance a bit more. From Table Top we go into this asana by extending your right arm and left leg back. Feel like you're reaching and stretching your spinal column towards your extended arm and leg. Hold for a couple breaths. Now switch sides. Repeat six times.

This pose works your stabilizing muscles and stretches the back.

Downward Facing Dog (AKA Down Dog): A classic well-known foundation pose that you might do a number of times in any given yoga session. Used as a transition between asanas.

1-Get on your hands and knees with your wrists positioned at the level of your shoulders and your knees under your hips (perpendicular).

2-Now curl your toes forward and push backwards while raising your knees off the board until your legs are straight and your butt is in the air forming a pyramid shape.

3-Push backwards more, and eventually with practice you'll be able to touch the board with your heels (flat footed).

Down Dog Pose

4-Now bend your knees, leaving your feet stationary while dropping your butt backwards and down to where your stomach touches or is close to touching your thighs. Then return to the pyramid position and repeat.

Down Dog opens up your back and works your thighs.

Low Lunge: From Down Dog you can work into this pose. Shift your position or pyramid so that your arms are aligned straight under your shoulders. Your face is now looking straight ahead as you move your left knee forward between your arms leaving your right knee/leg straight.

Low Lunge Pose

Your left knee should be under your chest and try to get your foot under the knee so your lower leg forms a right angle to the board. (Or as close as you can.) Now drop your right knee to the board as you raise your torso up as far as comfortable.

Raise your arms out to the side and then arc them upwards over your head with the palms touching. Now lift that right knee off the board and hold this pose for a couple seconds. You can raise and lower the right knee a few times then go back to Down Dog pose and lunge forward with your other leg switching sides. Repeat six times.

A variation of this is the **Twist and Low Lunge**. From Low Lunge twist your torso sideways with one arm reaching skyward and the other stabilizing on the board. Now switch sides and repeat six times.

This pose strengthens the lower body and lengthens the spine.

Twist & Low Lunge Pose

It also stretches the groin, legs and opens up your chest and hips.

Boat pose: Start from a seated position with legs flat on board. Now bring your legs up in the air about 45% off the board. Your torso will angle backwards at the same time but try and maintain

Boat Pose

Shoulder Stand Pose

your lower lumbar curve (don't slump). Your body now forms a "V" shape. Bring your arms straight out in front lining up with your shoulders. Too difficult? Bend your knees. Now hold for a few breaths, relax back to a seated position and repeat six times.

The Boat pose really works the abdominals.

Shoulder Stand pose: From a seated position lay your back down on the board. Raise your legs straight up into the air assisted by supporting and pushing with your hands behind your hips, fingers pointing skyward. The textbooks say your shoulders, hips and feet should be aligned vertically when you get into position but for most of us I think this tends to tweak the neck. So just focus on lining up your feet above your hips and tuck your hips as much above your shoulders as reasonable. Move your hands from behind your hips to your lower back to help out.

This pose helps stretch the neck and relax the lower back while loosening up the chest and shoulders. To lessen strain on the neck, ideally you place a folded towel under your shoulders (not the neck).

Corpse Pose

Corpse pose: Ah, at last a pose everyone can master. Lay flat on your board, backside down and relax. If you have a shirt handy cover your eyes and let your body sink into your board. Let everything drift away for a few meditative moments. This is a good way to wrap up your yoga sessions.

So you just finished a series of yoga poses and of course there's so much more to learn should you wish to take things further on your SUP.

SUP Fitness Paddling

Frankly this can be just about anything you like were you push it. You can keep it simple and just do sprints towards a buoy or anchored boat or do the same for time. These sprints might last anywhere from 1-4 minutes with a one minute rest in-between. You can mix up these short faster intervals with longer ones at a slower pace. Consider the shorter sprints to be anaerobic and the longer ones more on the aerobic level. You can choose a point to point course and see how you can improve your time with some training. And finally you can jump in some of the local races for fun. You can also get more serious with more formal training that will

SUP racing

include anaerobic and aerobic workouts to optimize your power for sudden sprints and your endurance for long distances.

Fitness racing equipment: As a beginning racer or someone who just wants to train to achieve a higher level of fitness you can use your existing SUP and paddle. However, if you begin to take racing more seriously you'll need to upgrade. I've mentioned before that racers generally use a slightly different length paddle than if they are simply touring. You also need to consider the stiffness of the shaft. For shorter races a stiffer shaft will give you more energy transfer but for longer races a shaft with more flex will help reduce muscle fatigue.

In terms of racing boards. There are many choices in respect to designs, lengths and weight. Most SUP races have several different categories that you can choose from. Below is a list of categories published by the World Paddling Association (WPA). In all of the categories listed there are no board weight or design restrictions.

#1 SUP Surfboard

Length 12' 2" ft. maximum

#2 SUP 12'6" Class

　　Length 12'6" ft. maximum

#3 SUP 14 ft. Class

　　Length 14 ft. maximum

#4 SUP Unlimited

　　Length-No length maximum

The racing SUP is a different beast than the flatwater or surfing SUP. Racing boards usually have what are called displacement hulls. The nose looks more like the prow of a ship with a vertical profile that cuts through the water rather than, for example, the flat nose of a surfboard which planes over the water. Racing boards have little or no rocker so they have longer waterlines relative to their given length. Take a 12 foot surfboard that has rocker (or curvature between the nose and tail to rise above the water, chop and waves) versus a 12 foot displacement hull race board, and the racer has more of its length in the water at any given time. This translates to

Racing SUP with concave deck for a firmer grip

more speed which is enhanced by the nose design and the light weight composition. The top racing SUPs are high end creatures made of carbon and or light weight composites. High end also means greater cost and a more fragile lay-up. Not a serious racer, don't buy one.

Training program: Here's an example of a one month training program I read about to get you going for your first race or simply

Displacement Hull Racing SUP

for your own fitness program. This program is courtesy of SUP instructor/trainer Garrett McCoy. First we'll discuss the different types of workouts you'll be doing.

Intervals-This is high intensity stuff. For example 10 x 1 minute sprints with a one minute break in-between aka 10:1:1.

Fartlek-This means paddling at a hard working pace (80% effort) for five minutes followed by a one minute sprint. 2-3 minute recovery in-between each set at cruising speed.

LSD-Just like in running you put in those long slow miles to build up endurance.

Added to this we'll throw in some one mile sprints at the top speed you can maintain for the mile.

Week #1 (3 workouts on separate days)- assume warm up/ warm down each time

Day 1-Intervals 10:1:1

Day 2-Fartlek 5:5:1 (that's 5 x 5 minutes each followed by a 1 minute sprint)

Day 3-LSD for 6 miles (depends on the race distance you're prepping for)

Week #2

Day 1-Intervals 8:2:1

Day 2-One mile sprints. You'll do four of these with 3-4 minute recovery aka 4:1:3/4

Day 3-LSD for 7 miles

Week #3

Day 1-Intervals 6:3:1

Day 2-Fartlek 6:4:1

Day 3-LSD for 6 miles

Week #4

Day 1-Intervals 12:1:1

Day 2-One mile sprints 4:1:3

Day 3-LSD for 8 miles

Keep in mind the above training regimen is just to give you a program to get going. It's a great idea if you can work out with someone who has more experience and learn from them. They'll also push you and at the same time you can start experimenting with drafting on their side and tail wake.

When you first start out doing a SUP race for fun you'll notice a few different forward stroke styles beyond what you've seen amongst the casual SUP tourers. Racers exaggerate the forward crunch at the catch to drive the paddle in quickly and give more power to the stroke. You might also see some racers adopting a surfer stance from time to time which allows for a longer and very powerful stroke called the *Plunge Stroke*. The debate is on over whether or not the plunge stroke gives you more power and speed than a stroke using a parallel stance. One argument is that since you paddle on the same side with the plunge stroke you reduce wasted time in switching sides. Of course, there are challenges to keeping your SUP running straight while paddling only on one side. The experts have developed ways to adjust their stroke to keep moving in a straight line, and some racers are now using angled fins to help out as well.

There's a few other things I'll discuss before we move on. People ask about stroke rates, board speed and how many hours to workout. In race situations you might have a stroke rate in the

Racing Stroke with aggressive forward crunch

The Plunge Stroke

mid-40s to low 50s per minute. If you are using the Tahitian style it would be a little faster. Your board speed, depending on your board type and abilities is about 5-6mph and doing downwind runs 10mph or greater. New paddlers might train from 4-8 hours a week. Intermediate paddlers 8-12 hours and experts more like 13-20 hours per week. It just depends on how hard core you want to get and what time you have available away from that thing called

Racers Drafting

work and family responsibilities.

This discussion hasn't really talked about dealing with wind, chop and swell as a racer. Simply put, one of the best ways to get more comfortable in adverse conditions is to spend time SUP surfing. Surf conditions will force you to improve your paddling skills, balance and comfort in swells, waves and chop. Surf conditions will also make you practice your low and high braces so you won't tip over and waste precious time in a race.

Finally, I'll suggest that you train in conditions that you think you might find on race day. If the location is prone to wind and chop you better be prepared to deal with this.

What's SUP?

Chapter 5   SUP Surfing

This chapter talks about SUP surfing for the beginner because the romantic allure of riding slow moving rollers with a sunset backdrop and dolphins frolicking away, will probably appeal to many of you.

SUP Surfing

Yep there's something about surfing that captures our imaginations. So if you're ready to give it a shot there's a few general rules of the road to pay attention to.

1-Dress for immersion since you'll be wiping out a lot. Unless you're in Hawaii this means a one-piece full wetsuit, maybe some booties and even a neoprene hood.

2-Choose mellow conditions meaning a location with small (2-3 foot) rolling waves with no major currents or submerged rocks or reefs. Pick an area away from other SUP surfers, regular surfers, kayakers etc. so you don't hit anyone. The reality is that when you ditch your board by diving off it into a wave, it's a big heavy tumbling object that can seriously hurt anyone in its path.

3-Be prepared. You should be a good swimmer and be comfortable in moderate wave conditions and of course physically fit.

4-Finally maintain awareness. A SUP is a hard object and your fin can cut you. Leashes can tangle you up. If you have a bad wipe out and feel the leash jerking at your leg know there might be some recoil. Come to the surface guarding your face and head. And yes, hopefully you're still clutching your paddle.

When you fall off your board dive away from the board and try to spear your paddle into the water keeping it away from your face and body without over extending your arm. Once submerged "ball up," that is roll into a ball as best you can while controlling your paddle. This position will help protect your spine, reduce your profile in terms of a wave tumbling you around, and help protect your body and face against possible impact with your board or someone elses.

In the surf zone the Coast Guard does not require you to wear a PFD. Generally speaking a PFD is considered more of a hazard in the surf zone than a benefit. But obviously this depends on the situation. If you are walking your board into the ocean and a smaller wave hits you one approach is to dive into the wave. This means you'll grab the nose of your SUP while lining up your paddle lengthwise to the board, and pushing down on the nose, dive into the wave and let the foam roll over you. Obviously, having a PFD on would inhibit your ability to dive. It's the same problem if you wipe out while surfing and you try and protect yourself by diving into the wave. Kind of tough with a lot of flotation strapped to your body. However, if your leash snaps, your board disappears and you are exhausted from all the fun that PFD will float you. At any rate there are always exceptions but generally you'll find that surfers and SUP surfers don't wear PFD's. But on flatwater it's required and people SUPing on rivers should also wear them.

As a beginner you can use the same board and paddle that you use on flatwater. Better to have a nice stable board. Here's a few sizing charts to give you the general picture.

Beginners   **Surf conditions 1-3 feet**

Board length 11'6"-12'6"   Width at least 30"

Intermediate   **Surf conditions 4-6 feet**

Board length 9'6" (lighter builds)   Width 28"

Board length 10'6" (heavier builds)   Width 30"

Advanced (big waves)*

Board length 11'3"-13'   Width 27-28"

*These boards are harder to ride because they are narrower but offer more control and speed, and can come with footstraps.

In terms of paddle sizing, stick with what you got but if you really get into SUP surfing eventually you'll use a paddle that's 6-8 inches above your height (flatwater goes 8-10 inches above height). The reason for the shorter paddle is that when surfing you are hunched over more for better control and stability, and hence a shorter paddle works best.

A note on leashes. As a beginner use what you have. But eventually you might get a leash that attaches around your upper calf below the knee. This solves two problems. It helps keep you from stepping on your leash, and your calf can take more punishment than if the leash is pulling violently at your ankle. Long board surfers and those on SUPs often choose this type because these bigger volume boards can create much greater tension on the leash. Finally, do you go with a coiled or uncoiled leash? There are plenty of mixed opinions on this. A good compromise is a leash that is part coiled and part flat (uncoiled).

Getting started: Stand on the shoreline for a while and check out the conditions. Where are the waves breaking and can you figure out the timing and the sets? If there's a lull between them that's a good time to paddle out. Carry your board out into knee deep water, and from here there are several approaches to get out beyond any small breaking waves. You can either lie in the prone position and use your arms to paddle out like a surfer or go to your "safety" or kneeling position. Obviously, the later will give you more speed but less stability. Finally, if you already have some experience

Sideways to the wave
bad positioning

and the waves are small you might be able to move to a standing position. Or you have to use all these positions depending on the circumstances to get out beyond the break.

Most importantly you don't want to get sideways to the waves because this is the quickest way to wipe out. Power through the

small waves if you're kneeling or standing, by planting your blade (reaching over the top of the wave if possible) and pulling yourself through and over. If you are in a standing position you might start off in a parallel stance but as a small wave approaches you'll drop one leg back into a surfer stance, putting a little weight on the tail to raise the nose as you power over a wave. Also bend your knees deeper so you are crouching for added stability. Once the wave goes by you can go back to the more stable parallel stance.

Inevitably you'll encounter a wave or series of waves which brings out the OMG factor. There are various strategies to call upon, the least effective being praying to the gods that you don't get hammered. Depending on the size of the wave and your abilities there are choices but figuring out the best approach is really experiential and you need to learn by doing. The traditional *duck dive* used by prone surfers where they slide to the front of their board and try and spear it downward into the wave face really doesn't work with the higher volume SUPs.

A choice that works with smaller waves that break gently is flipping the board upside down, called the *Turtle*. Here you let the force of the foam roll over the bottom of your board.

SUP Surfing

But ultimately if you can't power over or through a wave you might have to abandon ship which means diving away from your board, into the wave, while also spearing your paddle through it. Remember to *ball up*. As you surface protect your face/head as your leash might be under tension and snap your board back at you. Otherwise, once you surface quickly retrieve your board by pulling on the leash and climb back on.

Finally, you are ready to try surfing a wave. Start with small rolling waves that aren't breaking. One of the reasons SUP surfing is popular is because you have a better field of vision for hunting for waves and more speed to catch them. So those slow rolling waves that prone surfers can't catch are your domain.

Being able to turn quickly to meet the wave is critical. Drop one leg backwards to weight the tail and execute a pivot turn by sweeping your paddle on one side (low and wide). As you sweep your paddle behind you arc the blade around the tail for more turning power.

A good strategy is to take your first waves in the kneeling

position. You'll have a greater success rate and begin to figure out the mystery of catching waves. As the wave approaches start paddling to get some speed up. As it rolls under you take some quick short strokes, and when you feel you've caught the wave your choices are to simply go straight or cut left or right. On small waves you can often just ride straight ahead but on bigger waves you need to cut away from the section that is breaking.

For example, if the wave is breaking from right to left you will cut to the left. You'll be using your paddle for steering and balance. To help turn left execute a rudder stroke on the left side. You can also shift weight on the left rail. If you feel you're losing the wave use a rudder stroke on the right side, and this will turn you back into the deeper section of the wave.

When you've had some success riding waves from the kneeling position you're ready to try standing up. Once you've caught the wave shift into a surfer stance which will give you more control for turning.

Along with ruddering and leaning on the relative rail for directional control, you might need to shift your weight forward/backward on the board. If you feel the nose diving move back or vice a versa if you feel the tail is dragging and you're losing the wave.

Inevitably you'll either fall or take a more serious wipe out. If it's a small wave and a gentle fall, sometimes you can grab the rail with one hand and fall over the back of the wave and maintain control of your board. But maybe you're more out of control. Protect yourself as mentioned before by falling away from the board and diving into the wave so you don't get swept down wave and into your board. Remember, you've got to also hold onto your paddle and position it so it doesn't clobber your body or face. Mostly you want to avoid falling or being in a position with your board between you and a wave as this will cause a nasty collision.

Now scramble back on your board and look for your next wave.

Chapter 6   Transporting Your SUP

The object of this chapter is to give you some immediate feedback on how to safely transport your SUP as well as how to carry it down to the water. Although I want to keep this part simple and inexpensive for you I'll give you some ideas on the various options available. So you can keep it simple, spend minimal amounts of money or open up your wallet and buy all the new gadgets.

Transport by vehicle

Assuming you need to transport your SUP a fair distance the easiest way is via your vehicle. Let's assume you have a rack system on the roof which is either factory installed or an add-on. What we are looking for basically is a roof rack with two crossbars, spaced hopefully, at least three to four feet apart. If you have this then the rest is simple.

Find something to pad the crossbars to protect your board. Usually you can go to a hardware store and get some closed cell pipe insulation to wrap around the bars. Or maybe you have an old style foam sleeping pad that you can cut up. Just throw a couple wraps of duct tape around the padding so it doesn't fly off the crossbars when your board is not mounted.

Board orientation: The next issue is much debated. How to line up your board on top of your vehicle? I've read up on the subject and there's seems to be some consensus that the best way in terms of aero-dynamics is to load your board on top with the tail facing forward and the fin pointing towards the sky. The reason for this is due to something called lift as in what happens with an airplane wing. It is argued by the techies that if you put the nose to the front with the board deck down it acts like a wing. Therefore it creates more torque on your straps and rack system and lowers gas mileage.

So if you want to be aerodynamic, fin up, tail forward although frankly I think this looks a little odd. But it does offer some safety

benefits. For one, if your straps or tie- downs loosen and the board slides backwards, the fin will probably catch the strap and keep the board from flying into the car behind you. Also, this enables you to loop a line through the leash plug, securing your bow to the front fender, so that if your rack systems fails the board won't go flying backwards. It's what kayakers do. In fact, they take it one step further and have a bowline and a stern line in addition to the lines around the kayak and crossbars.

Also, in terms of distance and gas mileage concerns it's generally thought that it is better to have less of the board hanging in front of the windshield and more hanging off the back.

All this said if you are traveling shorter distances such as twenty miles and less, it really doesn't matter how you load your board, fin up or down, or tail to the front or back as long as it is strapped down securely. The tie down jobs I see the most position the tail to the rear fin up, although again this isn't the most aerodynamic.

Tie down straps: My favorite way to tie a board down onto the crossbars is by using cam straps. These are straps with cam

buckles and it's an added plus if the cam buckles are padded so you don't ding your car paint. In lieu of cam straps you can use rope or line that's rated for a lot of torque. But I would stay away from bungee type tie downs. It's a dangerous weapon when stretched and you can knock out your own tooth when it goes flying. Some people will buy one long cam strap, let's say a twenty footer and weave it around the board and both crossbars. I'm in favor of having two separate straps, one per bar. If one strap fails you still have one holding the board down.

For each crossbar do the same. Take your cam strap and loop it around the bar on the inside side of your SUP. Now run the cam buckle end and the other end over your board and loop the non-buckle end under the cross bar inside of the tower (that way it can't slide off if it loosens somehow). The cam buckle end will be on top of the board within reach. Now feed the strap end through the buckle and tighten. You'll have to position the buckle so it doesn't dig into the board when tightened, and it's best to avoid the rail. Again there's less worry if the cam buckle comes padded.

If you want to protect against the quick snatch and run you can buy a **SUP rack locking system**. One such system, priced around $200, can be fit on your existing rack bars without any tools. The more expensive systems like this can hold two boards, and come with adjustable padded cradles for a custom fit. The straps that tie-down your SUP have a steel cable running through them and secure

SUP Lock-Down System

into locking cams. A thief would have to either pop the cam-lock or cut the cable which would require wire cutters.

Tying down two boards: If you want things to look nice and symmetrical take the fin off the bottom board. Load and position this as mentioned above, tail forward, fin box facing up. Now you want to place a couple foam blocks in-between the boards so there's no rubbing. You can make these or buy these. If you make them cut something that's 1-2 inches thick, about 20" inches wide and 3-4" deep. Space these out and make sure the boards are not

rubbing when you load up the second board. If you leave the fin on the bottom board obviously the boards will have to be slightly offset. If you are traveling a long distance take the time to take both fins off. This way you'll have a nice neatly stacked package and less drag. Using your cam straps tie down as discussed above.

Other options: As mentioned earlier there are a plethora of rack systems depending on your vehicle type. You just have to do the legwork to figure out which one to get. If you happen to have a station wagon or something similar you might be able to load your board inside with it sticking out the back. Just make sure you have padding for any contact points, and that it is tied securely so that when you hit the brakes it won't go flying out. If you have a truck with just a cab there are rack systems were a single crossbar can go over the cab and you mount a post with a crossbar inserted into your hitch. This gives you a stable platform to lay your board on and to tie it down. The list is endless! In fact there's something called the **HandiRack** which is an inflatable crossbar systems for use on cars that don't have a rack system. For example a rental car. The

inflatable crossbars go over the roof and the straps wrap around inside the car. This can be used as a quick rack system for any car that has four doors and it will carry SUPs and even kayaks.

Other carrying options: If the weather is nice and you're not that far from the put in why not use your bike to transport your SUP. There are a variety of systems to do so. The **Mule Transport System** is one example. In this system you strap wheels around the tail end and these are held secure via a strap system that connects

to something that wraps around the nose. There's a way to then strap this onto your bike seat and away you go. You can also use the same system when walking your board to the water over just about any terrain.

Most typically though you have to get your board from the car top to the water. Again there are wheel systems if the board is too heavy for you. Otherwise you'll just carry your board. A lot of boards these days are manufactured with handles inset into the mid-point of the board. If they are set right the board balances nicely. If your board does not have a handle be it inset or not there are plenty of after-market handles. A typical style is a glue mount type handle. Even if you have a carrying handle some people find carrying the board challenging for all but short distances. A typical board has some weight to it, and frankly all that weight seems to concentrate on tugging at your fingers and wrists. One way to deal with this is to purchase an over the shoulder carrying system. There's one system called the **Big Board Schlepper** with adjustments to fit a variety of sized boards. The straps wrap around the board and the weight is carried by your shoulders instead of your hands and arms. Systems like this also usually have smaller straps to hold your paddle as you walk down to the water.

Board Storage

The great thing about storing your board is that it doesn't have the weight of let's say a kayak. Maybe you've noticed plastic kayaks with dimpled hulls before. This usually comes from being on a rack with a couple crossbars and add to this some hot weather and the kayak will sag. SUPs on the other hand are relatively light and stiff so this is not an issue. Ideally you store your board indoors which protects it against the elements, namely the sun. If you have a flat surface lay the board on this (fin up), but a rack system or standing

Board bag protects during transport & storage

the board on edge over some padding can work. Or hang it from the rafters in your garage.

I'd recommend a board bag to protect against the sun if you're storing your SUP outdoors. An added advantage to having a board bag is that it's a great way to transport your SUP. When your board is strapped down to your car racks the board bag protects your board against possible dings from any airborne projectiles like rocks thrown up by that big truck in front of you. If left outside always tie down your board in case of wind.

Made in the USA
San Bernardino, CA
21 December 2016